Super Sonic Logos

Super Sonic Logos

The Power of Audio Branding

David Allan, PhD

BUSINESS EXPERT PRESS

Leader in applied, concise business books

Quotes

"*Written in an engaging and accessible style, Allan takes a deep dive into the world of sonic branding, with a particular emphasis on sonic logos— the sound signatures that serve as the 'voice' of the brands they represent. This is formidable work of scholarship, laden with practical wisdom, and a welcome addition to the literature in this emerging area of marketing.*"
—**James J. Kellaris, Composer, musician, and Womack/Gemini Professor of Marketing at the University of Cincinnati**

"*Of all the distinctive sonic assets available to brands, the sonic logo is certainly one of the hardest working. In "Super Sonic Logos," Allan explores these small but mighty sonic signatures. From the three notes of the NBC chime to the five notes of the Intel bong, David educates and entertains with a behind the scenes look into the history and creation of some of the most iconic sonic logos in the world. Ba da ba BA ba—I'm lovin' it.*"—**Steve Keller, Sonic Strategy Director, Studio Resonate, SXM Media**

"*Sound powerfully affects us all, even though most of us—and most brands— are unconscious of this. Great brands deliver consistent experience in all the senses, so they design for the ears as well as the eyes. That's why sonic logos have become so potent and so vital for every brand to consider. This book records in detail how some of the world's greatest sonic logos came about, making it an invaluable guide for any brand that wants to form a deeper emotional connection with its audience using the power of sound.*"—**Julian Treasure, Chairman, The Sound Agency**

Description

This book looks at the best of the best of sonic logos from the people who gave them notes. Whether you consider them to be music to your ears or *earworms*, these are the ten most **note**worthy sonic logos of all time and one future hall of famer. So open your computer and meet Water Werzowa the creator of the Intel logo and Brian Eno who gave Windows 95 sound.

Remember your favorite television show or movie and say hello to Mike Post from Law and Order fame, Dr. James "Andy" Moore from THX and John Williams who scared us in Jaws...and don't forget to honor those NBC chimes.

Keep your phone on in case you get a ring from Lance Massey on your T-Mobile or Joel Beckerman on your AT&T commercial. And if you get hungry, there's always something from McDonald's courtesy of Bill Lamar or a Coke from Joe Belliotti and Umut Ozaydini. Finally, pay for it all with your Raja Rajamannar's Mastercard.

Keywords

audio; branding; logos; sonic

Punch, brothers! Punch with care!
Punch in the presence of the passenjare!
—Mark Twain, "A Literary Nightmare," 1876

"A Literary Nightmare" is a short story written by Mark Twain in 1876. The story is about Twain's encounter with an *earworm*, or virus-like jingle, and how it occupies his mind for several days until he manages to "infect" another person, thus removing the jingle from his mind. The story was also later published under the name "Punch, Brothers, Punch!"

Special thanks to Michael J. Morris for his support of this book.

Contents

First Note

What's this book about? First, let's start with the title. "Super" suggests excellence. "Sonic" means sound. "Logo" is a symbol. Put them together and you can hear the power of audio branding. Next, a brief background into audio branding especially logos might help. Audio branding is not new. Neither are audio logos. What is new is an appreciation of sound. Not surprising that sound is riding the wave of smart speakers. Houses are becoming more voice-activated every day turning on lights and sound. We are telling Alexa and Google daily to play our favorite music and podcasts while we buy our groceries and clothes. By the end of 2021, that number is predicted to grow to 23.5 million.[1] Voice shopping is also expected to jump to $40 billion in 2022.[2] Even though new audio logos are being turned on every day, it may indeed still be "the dawn of the audio logo."[3] The father of "atmospherics" Philip Kotler (1973) believes that today's atmospherics (sound) must be designed for devices as well as spaces.[4] Sound has always been and continues to be a powerful atmospheric for not just marketing but also movies, television, media, and sports. It is clearly the time for brands to turn up the volume on audio branding because "brands without an audio presence will have no presence."[5]

But what really is audio branding?

The American Marketing Association defines audio branding as "the approach of using unique, proprietary sound and music to convey a brand's essence and values. Just as visual branding defines a brand using color and shape, audio branding defines a brand through sound and music."[6] The power of "sonic branding is twofold: the creation of brand expressions in sound and the consistent, strategic usage of these properties across touchpoints."[7] These marketing *touchpoints* open new lines of communication and can give the brand a deeper voice. "If a brand can identify opportunities for sonic communications and applies some of the art of sonic branding, it gains access to a whole world of communication opportunities that it never had before."[8] It can be heard in both advertising and media. "The development of the marketing and (television and) movie industries over the last 100 years informs much of what we call sonic branding."[9] Sonic branding can be better and cheaper for the brand in the long run because "if a brand-owner has the foresight to commission their own sonic branding, then they have the right to expect that they will not be held to ransom by limited (synchronization) licenses."[10]

And what is an audio logo?

An audio logo can be considered a brand's musical *nickname*. "The audio logo represents the acoustic identifier of a brand and it is often combined with an (animated) visual logo. It should be distinct/unique, recognizable, flexible, memorable and fit the brand by reflecting brand attributes."[11] It has "a powerful sonic mnemonic function."[12] It is "a vessel for associations."[13] It is different from a jingle which is "a short slogan, verse or tune designed to be easily remembered and a mnemonic intended to help the memory."[14] A sonic logo is notes not words (although sometimes the notes provide the instrumental for the melody) that the brand commissions and can own copyrights. It typically is between three to six notes with limited research that suggests that six is optimal to influence a consumer's willingness to buy.[15] Sonic logos "convey values and principles brands want to be seen (and heard) to stand for."[16]

Sonic logos have two primary jobs: "the heraldic function of drawing the listener's attention to whatever the logo is a logo for, whether a product or a service, a company or some other organization, or a radio or television programme; and an identity function, expressing the values and principles which that product or service, or other entity, stands for."[17] Sonic logos

> combine a practical function with the expression of identity. Their functional structure is quite stable and homogeneous, calling the listener to attention through a melodic structure categorized by ascending melodies, large intervals, dotted rhythms, a lack of resolution, so that the music has an open ending, continuing in what

follows, whether it be a news bulletin or a work session of the computer user. The identity function is less stable and more varied and flexible, able to respond to new trends as they occur and primarily carried by timbres, often created through blending sounds with specific meaning potentials or cultural references into novel "composites of connotations." Sonic logos therefore embody both continuity and change, both generic homogeneity and stylistic variety.[18]

Sonic logos can be

even more powerful when they are tied to anthems or themes. An anthem is the long-form expression of a nation, a brand, a personal story, a movement, or a cause told in the language of sound. It expresses values in a sort of ownable sonic DNA. That DNA can then be used to make shorter sounds—sonic logos—that instantly and efficiently let listeners recall and understand rich stories.[19]

Is audio the same as sonic?

For our purposes, "sonic" and "sound" mean the same thing. Sonic *is* probably "sexier"[20] and more powerful. And sonic logos have been around forever. As Julian Treasure tells it:

Sonic logos have actually been around for hundreds of years: street calling used to be the main way tradesman advertised their services, as romanticised in the film Oliver. The modern-day equivalent is the ice cream van: just watch the cathartic effect of its chimes on surrounding buildings on a hot Summer's day to see the potency of sonic logos deployed in the right place at the right time. As soon as sound recording became viable, the advertising industry saw the potential of memorable music/voice combinations and the jingle and tagline were born. The dividing line between jingle or tagline and a sonic logo is blurred. In general, jingles and taglines come and go with campaigns, or are specific to them, and rarely live for more than a few years. Some taglines are so strong they become sonic logos (Tony the Tiger's "they're gr-r-r-r-reat!"). Tony notwithstanding, it wasn't until the 1990s that sonic logos started to be taken seriously and their use came to be considered by major brands as a matter of course. The real sea change came with Intel.[21]

Now, on to the book!

It all began with the NBC Chimes. And that is where we begin with a deep dive into the best of the best sonic logos. The ones we can't get out of heads. Whether you consider them to be music to your ears or *earworms*,[22] these are the ten most *noteworthy* sonic logos of all time and the people who gave them the *notes*. It's the backstory behind the logo historically and then in most cases from the creators themselves. Some of the interviews were done today (recently) and when they could not they are from interviews yesterday (before). You will meet John Williams, yes that John Williams, who in 1975 with just two notes made us scared to go back into the water (*Jaws*). Then turn on the television to get locked in with Mike Post and just one of his countless themes from *Law and Order* (You thought I was going to say *Hill Street Blues*, didn't you? He did that too!). After that, it is off to Austria and maybe the most famous sonic logo of all time from Intel and its creator Walter Werzowa. From there we meet the man who owned a Mac but gave Window's 95 its voice, Brian Eno. If you have a phone ringing, it's probably Lance Massey (T-Mobile) or Joel Beckerman (AT&T). If you are hungry better eat something before you meet Bill Lamar (McDonald's) or Joe Belliotti and Umut Ozaydini (Coca-Cola). Finally, you'll hear from a future Hall of Famer, Raja Rajamannar (Mastercard). What will you learn from this book? That every great sonic logo begins with a note.

CHAPTER 1

NBC (1950)

Courtesy of **NBCUNIVERSAL Media, LLC**

Three notes. N-B-C. The godfather of sonic logos. It has stood the test of time. In 1950,[1] we know that the NBC chimes ("G-E-C") became the first "purely audible" service mark[2] (any word, name, symbol, or device, or any combination thereof) granted by the U.S. Patent and Trademark Office.[3] It became the first sound mark. "A sound mark identifies and distinguishes a product or service through audio rather than visual means.

Examples of sound marks include: (1) a series of tones or musical notes, with or without words, and (2) wording accompanied by music."[4]

The back story for the chimes' "G-E-C" sequence is that it comes from the initials of the General Electric Company (GE). In 1987, Robert C. Wright, the president and CEO of NBC, testified before the U.S. Congress that "Not everyone knows that GE was one of the original founders of RCA, NBC's former parent, and that the notes of the famous NBC chimes are G-E-C, standing for the General Electric Company."[5] The sound mark was originally issued to General Electric Broadcasting.[6] The official description, as recorded by its registration at the U.S. Patent and Trademark Office, is:

> The mark comprises a sequence of chime-like musical notes which are in the key of C and sound the notes G, E, C, the "G" being the one just below middle C, the "E" the one just above middle C, and the "C" being middle C, thereby to identify applicant's broadcasting service.[7]

United States Patent Office

916,522

Registered July 13, 1971

PRINCIPAL REGISTER
Service Mark

Ser. No. 349,496, filed Jan. 23, 1970

THE MARK COMPRISES
THE MUSICAL NOTES
G, E, C PLAYED ON
CHIMES

National Broadcasting Company, Inc. (Delaware corporation)
30 Rockefeller Plaza
New York, N.Y. 10020

For: BROADCASTING OF TELEVISION PROGRAMS, in CLASS 104 (INT. CL. 38).

First use at least as early as Sept. 9, 1961; in commerce at least as early as Sept. 9, 1961.

The mark comprises a sequence of chime-like musical notes which are in the key of C and sound the notes G, E, C, the "G" being the one just below middle C, the "E" the one just above middle C, and the "C" being middle C, thereby to identify applicant's broadcasting service.

Owner of Reg. No. 523,616.

NBC Chimes sound trademark, Serial No. 72349496, Registration No. 0916522

The original filing it said:

A sound mark depends upon aural perception of the listener which may be as fleeting as the sound itself unless, of course, the sound is so inherently different or distinctive that it attaches to the subliminal mind of the listener to be awakened when heard and to be associated with the source or event with which it is struck. With "unique, different, or distinctive sounds." That "consumers "recognize and associate the sound with the offered services . . . exclusively with a single, albeit anonymous, source.[8]

History

We know that on November 29, 1929, the NBC Chimes sounded for the first time (at 59 minutes 30 seconds, and 29 minutes 30 seconds past the hour). But the inspiration and creation of the notes depends on who you are asking.

The earliest known sound recording of a musical dinner chime being used to identify a local radio station is that of WSB Atlanta. The radio voice of *The Atlanta Journal*, WSB signed on the air on March 15, 1922. Two of the station's earliest stars were the twin sisters Kate and Nell Pendley; according to Cox Broadcasting's history of WSB Welcome South, Brother, published in 1974, WSB manager Lambdin Kay was looking for a distinctive identification to close each program, and Nell Pendley offered him her Deagan Dinner Chimes. Kay created an identifier by ringing the notes E–C–G, the first three notes of the popular WWI song "Over There" and WSB in Atlanta in addition to being the first station to adopt a three-chime signature, it was directly responsible for NBC's chimes. This explanation states that, as an NBC affiliate, WSB was hosting a network broadcast of a Georgia Tech college football game, and NBC staff at the network's New York City headquarters heard the WSB chimes, which prompted them to ask permission to adopt it for use by the national networks.[9]

An alternative birthplace involves WJZ.

In July of 1921, RCA bought WJZ from Westinghouse, and five years later, in July of 1926, they bought WEAF from AT&T. The National Broadcasting Company was incorporated by RCA on September 8, 1926, and two months later, on November 15, the NBC Radio Network debuted. In those early days, at the end of a programs, the NBC announcer would read the call letters of all the NBC stations carrying the program. As the network added more stations this became impractical and would cause some confusion among the affiliates as to the conclusion of network programming and when the station break should occur on the hour and half-hour. Some sort of coordinating signal was needed to signal the affiliates for these breaks and allow each affiliate to identify. Three men at NBC were given the task of finding a solution to the problem and coming up with such a coordinating signal. These men were; Oscar (O.B.) Hanson, from NBC engineering, Earnest LaPrada, an NBC orches- tra leader, and Phillips Carlin, an NBC announcer. During the years 1927 and 1928 these men experimented with a seven note sequence of chimes, G-C-G-E-G-C-E, which proved too complicated for the announcers to consistently strike in the correct order. Sometime later they came up with the three note G-E-C combination.[10]

Now you know that the only thing that is clear about the origination of the NBC Chimes are the notes G-E-C and its longevity. The takeaway from this sonic logo is that sometimes the simple things in life and logos are the most memorable.

CHAPTER 2

JAWS (1975)

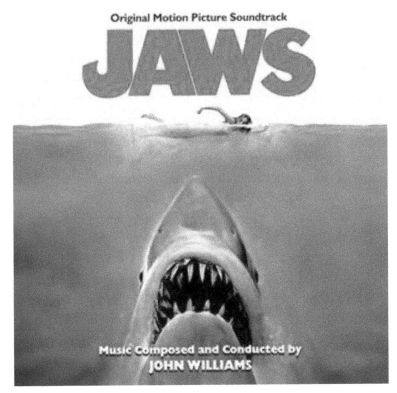

Courtesy of Universal Studios Licensing LLC

Before Shark Week, there was Jaws and that music. "F to F sharp. With those two notes, composer John Williams ensured that venturing into water would never feel safe again."[1] Meet John Williams who used a lot of instruments to introduce a mechanical shark and the rest is history.

Rarely have six basses, eight celli, four trombones and a tuba held more power over listeners. Especially in a movie theatre. John Williams's score for Jaws ranks as some of the most terrifying music ever written for the cinema. The music of Jaws was as responsible as filmmaker Steven Spielberg's imagery for scaring people out of the water in the summer of 1975. Its sheer intensity and visceral power helped to make the film a global phenomenon; Spielberg compared it to Bernard Herrmann's equally frightening, indelible music for Alfred Hitchcock's *Psycho* (1960). Williams viewed Spielberg's thriller about a giant Great White shark terrorising New England beachgoers as a chance for music to make a major contribution. First to come—and the only music that Williams demonstrated for Spielberg prior to the recording sessions—was the shark motif. "I played him the simple little E-F-E-F bass line that we all know on the piano," and Spielberg laughed at first. But, as Williams explained, "I just began playing around with simple motifs that could be distributed in the orchestra, and settled on what I thought was the most powerful thing, which is to say the simplest. Like most ideas, they're often the most compelling." According to Williams, Spielberg's response was: "Let's try it." *Jaws* not only became the highest-grossing film of its time; it propelled John Williams into the front rank of modern film composers. He won his second Academy Award for the score as well as a Golden Globe, a Grammy, and BAFTA's Anthony Asquith Award for film music. As Spielberg later put it: "I think the score was clearly responsible for half of the success of that movie."[2]

(By permission: Limelight Arts Media Pty Ltd (c))

In a career that spans five decades, John Williams has become one of America's most accomplished and successful composers for film and for the concert stage. Williams has composed the music and served as music director for more than one hundred films. His 40-year artistic partnership with director Steven Spielberg has resulted in many of Hollywood's most acclaimed and successful films, including *Schindler's List, E.T.: The Extra-Terrestrial, Jaws, Jurassic Park, Close Encounters of the Third Kind*, four Indiana Jones films, *Saving Private Ryan, Amistad, Munich, Hook, Catch Me If You Can, Minority Report, A.I.: Artificial Intelligence, Empire of the Sun, The Adventures of Tintin, and War Horse.* Williams has composed the scores for all of George Lucas' Star Wars films, the first three Harry Potter films, *Superman: The Movie, JFK, Born on the Fourth of July, Memoirs of a Geisha, Far and Away, The Accidental Tourist, Home Alone, Nixon, The Patriot, Angela's Ashes, Seven Years in Tibet, The Witches of Eastwick, Rosewood, Sleepers, Sabrina, Presumed Innocent, The Cowboys,* and *The Reivers,* among many others. Williams has received five Academy Awards and 50 Oscar nominations, making him the Academy's most-nominated living person and the second-most nominated person in the history of the Oscars. He also has received seven British Academy Awards (BAFTA), 22 Grammys, four Golden Globes, five Emmys, and numerous gold and platinum records.[3]

On January 10, 1977, during the final days of the Ford administration, John Williams began writing music for *Star Wars*, a forthcoming sci-fi adventure film created by George Lucas. More than forty-two years later, on November 21, 2019, Williams presided over the final recording session for *The Rise of Skywalker*, the ninth and ostensibly last installment of the main *Star Wars* saga. Williams scored every film in the series, and there is no achievement quite like it in movie history, or, for that matter, in musical history. Williams composed more than twenty hours of music for the cycle, working with five different directors. He developed a library of dozens of distinct motifs, many of them instantly recognizable to a billion or more people. The *Star Wars* scores have entered the repertories of the most venerable orchestras around the world. When, earlier this year, Williams made his début conducting the Vienna Philharmonic, several musicians asked him for autographs. Williams is a courtly, soft-voiced, inveterately self-effacing man of eighty-eight. He is well aware of the extraordinary worldwide impact of his *Star Wars* music—not to mention his scores for *Jaws, Close Encounters of the Third Kind, E.T.,* the "Indiana Jones" movies, the "Harry Potter" movies, the "Jurassic Park" movies, and dozens of other blockbusters—but he makes no extravagant claims for his music, even if he allows that some of it could be considered "quite good." A lifelong workhorse, he resists looking back and immerses himself in the next task. In the coronavirus period, he has been at home, on the west side of Los Angeles, focusing on a new concert work—a concerto, for the violinist Anne-Sophie Mutter, which will have its première next year. In February, I visited Williams in his bungalow office on the Universal Studios back lot—part of an adobe-style complex belonging to Amblin Entertainment, Steven Spielberg's production company. Spielberg's office is nearby. The two men first worked together on *The Sugarland Express*, in 1974, and have collaborated on twenty-eight films to date—all but four of Spielberg's features. At a tribute, in 2012, Spielberg said, "John Williams has been the single most significant contributor to my success as a filmmaker." It is, however, *Star Wars* that anchors the composer's fame. Williams poured himself a glass of water in the bungalow kitchenette, settled into a chair in front of his desk, and addressed the topic of the *Star Wars* cycle. He is a tall man, still physically vigorous, his face framed by a trim, vaguely clerical white beard. "Thinking about it, and trying to speak about it, connects us with the idea of trying to understand time," he said. "How do you understand forty years? I mean, if someone said to you, 'Alex, here's a project. Start on it, spend forty years on it, see where you get'? Mercifully, I had no idea it was going to be forty years. I was not a youngster when I started, and I feel, in retrospect, enormously fortunate to have had the energy to be able to finish it—put a bow on it, as it were." In the mid-1970s, when Williams formed links to the young blockbuster directors Spielberg and Lucas, he was already well established in Hollywood. He was, in a sense, born into the business; his father, Johnny Williams, was a percussionist who played in the Raymond Scott Quintette and later performed on movie soundtracks. Williams worked several times with Bernard Herrmann, perhaps the greatest American film composer, celebrated for his scores for *Citizen Kane*, *Vertigo*, *Psycho*, and *Taxi Driver*. Williams, who sometimes joined his father at rehearsals, told me, "Benny liked the way my father played the timpani. 'Old Man Williams isn't afraid to break the head,' he'd say. Benny was a famously irascible character, but in later years he was always very encouraging to me. One time he got irritated was when I arranged 'Fiddler on the Roof.' 'Write your own music,' he said." The Williamses moved from the New York area to Los Angeles in 1947, when John was fifteen. A skilled pianist, he won notice for organizing a jazz group with classmates from North Hollywood High; a brief piece in Time referred to him as

Curley Williams. In 1955, he went to New York and studied at Juilliard with the great piano pedagogue Rosina Lhévinne. "It became clear," he says, "that I could write better than I could play." He composed his first feature-film score in 1958, for a race-car comedy called *Daddy-O*. Because of his skills as a jazz stylist and as a song arranger, he specialized at first in such comedic fare—other assignments included *Gidget Goes to Rome* and *Not with My Wife, You Don't!*—but he branched out into Westerns and period dramas. Recordings of two of his scores, for *The Reivers* and *The Cowboys*, fell into the hands of the young Spielberg, who was working as a writer and as a television director. When Spielberg undertook his first major theatrical film, *The Sugarland Express*, in 1974, he informed the studio that he wanted to collaborate with the composer of *The Reivers*. Williams told me, "I met what looked to be this seventeen-year-old kid, this very sweet boy, who knew more about film music than I did—every Max Steiner and Dimitri Tiomkin score. We had a meeting in a fancy Beverly Hills restaurant, arranged by executives. It was very cute—you had the feeling Steven had never been in a restaurant like that before. It was like having lunch with a teen-age kid, but a brilliant one." After *Sugarland* came *Jaws*. As Spielberg happily acknowledged, Williams's two-note double-bass ostinato played a crucial role in that movie's colossal success, particularly when mechanical-shark malfunctions left it to the composer to evoke the murderous beast at full power. Williams went on, "One day, Steven called me and said, 'Do you know George Lucas?' I said, 'No, I have no idea who he is.' 'Well, he's got this thing called "Star Wars," and he wants to have a classical'—his term, he didn't say Romantic—'classical score, and I've convinced George he should meet you, because he admired the score for *Jaws*.' I came out here one night, to Universal Studios, and met George." As Williams remembers it, Lucas had been entertaining the idea of using preexisting classical works on the *Star Wars* soundtrack. The composer argued for an original score, in which newly created themes could be manipulated and developed to best serve the drama. Lucas, through a representative, says that he never intended to use extant music in the film. What's not in doubt is that the director wanted a soundtrack with an old-Hollywood atmosphere, in keeping with the film's reliance on chivalric swashbuckler tropes. When Williams set to work in the second week of January 1977—he gave me the date after consulting an old diary—he fell back on the techniques of golden-age Hollywood: brief, sharply defined motifs; brilliant, brassy orchestration; a continuous fabric of underscoring. The film-music scholar Emilio Audissino has described the *Star Wars* score and others by Williams as "neoclassical," meaning that they draw on a sumptuously orchestrated style associated with such Central European émigrés as Steiner and Erich Wolfgang Korngold. "Neoclassical" is a better label than "neo-Romantic," since Williams is so steeped in mid-twentieth-century influences: jazz, popular standards, Stravinsky, and Aaron Copland, among others. When he writes for a Wagnerian or Straussian orchestra, he airs out the textures and gives them rhythmic bounce. *The Imperial March*, from *The Empire Strikes Back*, for example, has a bright, brittle edge, with skittering figures in winds and strings surrounding an expected phalanx of brass. The nine *Star Wars* scores make use of a vast library of leitmotifs—more than sixty of them, according to the scholar Frank Lehman. I showed Williams a copy of Lehman's "Complete Catalogue of the Musical Themes of 'Star Wars,' " which left him a bit nonplussed. ("Oh, wow," he said, paging through it. "How exhausting.") Talk of leitmotifs leads inevitably to the topic of Richard Wagner, with whom they are inextricably associated. Williams leaned back in his chair and smiled ruefully. "Well, I saw the 'Ring' at the Hamburg Opera, years ago, and found it somewhat inaccessible, mostly because I didn't know German," he said. "I don't really know the Wagner operas at all. If Mr. Hanslick were alive, I think I'd be sitting on the side of Brahms in the debate." (The Viennese critic Eduard Hanslick campaigned for Brahms and against Wagner in the late nineteenth century.) "People say they hear Wagner in 'Star Wars,' and I can only think, It's not because I put it there. Now, of course, I know that Wagner had a great influence on Korngold and all the early Hollywood composers. Wagner lives with us here—you can't escape it. I have been in the big river swimming with all of them." Wagnerian or not, Williams's leitmotifs have had an uncanny effect on audiences, stretching across generations. In the recent *Star Wars* movies, citations of the themes for the Force, Princess Leia, and Darth Vader bring listeners back not only to earlier moments in the cycle but to earlier moments in their lives. I felt this vividly when I saw *The Rise of Skywalker* at the Uptown, in Washington, DC; I had seen the first film there forty-two years earlier, when I was nine. Williams nodded when I told him this: he has heard many stories like it. "It's a little bit like how the olfactory system is wired with memory, so that a certain smell makes you remember your grandmother's cooking," he said. "A similar thing happens with music. Really, at the root of the question is something about our physiological or neurological setup we don't understand. It has to do with survival, or protection of group identity, or God knows what. Music can be so powerful, even though it wafts away and we chase it." Williams's most vivid memories of the first *Star Wars* score involve the recording sessions, with the London Symphony: "That fanfare at the beginning, I think it's the last thing I wrote. It's probably a little overwritten—I don't know. The thirty-second notes in the trombones are hard to get, in that register of the trombone. And the high trumpet part! Maurice Murphy, the great trumpet player of the L.S.O.—that first day of recording was actually his first day with the orchestra, and the first thing he played was that high C. There was a kind of team roar when he hit it perfectly. He's gone now, but I love that man." John Gracie, another longtime British trumpeter, remembers calling Murphy and asking how things were going at the new job. "Oh, all right," Murphy answered. "We're recording the music for a film with a big bear in it." After *Star Wars*, Williams emerged as the musical magus of the Hollywood blockbuster, his indelible themes glinting through high-tech spectacle. They were the product of long, solitary labor. "One of the things I have felt, rightly or not, was that these tunes or themes or leitmotifs in film at least need to be pretty—not accessible, but succinct," he said. "Eighty or ninety per cent of the attention is focussed elsewhere. The music has to cut through this noise of effects. So, O.K., it's going to be tonal. It's going to be D major. The tunes need to speak probably in a matter of seconds—five or six seconds." After casting another quizzical glance at Frank Lehman's catalogue of leitmotifs, Williams went on, "Whether I've been as successful with the new ones as with the old ones, I don't know. What I can tell you is that these genuine, simple tunes are the hardest things to uncover, for any composer. When Elgar or Beethoven finally finds one—I hope you'll pardon me if it sounds like I'm comparing myself to these people, but it might illustrate the point—in both cases, they understood what they had. Things that may seem more interesting, more harmonically attractive, don't quite do the job. And so you end up—as a film composer, at least—not always doing what you initially set out to do. People assume it's what you wanted to write, but it's what you needed to write." I asked him whether he had any personal favorites among his Hollywood scores—especially the less renowned ones. He told me, "Years ago, I did a film called 'Images' for Robert Altman, and the score used all kinds of effects for piano, percussion, and strings. It had a debt to Varèse, whose music enormously interested me. If I had never written film scores, if I had proceeded writing concert music, it might have been in this vein. I think I would have enjoyed it. I might even have been fairly good at it. But my path didn't go that way." In truth, Williams has built up a fairly large body of concert pieces. His new violin concerto, for Mutter, is eagerly awaited, because his first effort in the form—completed in 1976, just before the music for *Star Wars* and *Close Encounters*—is one of his most formidable creations. It was composed as a memorial to his first wife, the actress and singer Barbara Ruick, who died in 1974, of a cerebral hemorrhage. (Since 1980, he has been married to the photographer Samantha Winslow.) The language of the concerto leans toward Bartókian, mid-century modernism, though it is shot through with lyrical strains. Williams excels at the concerto form; he has also written a harmonically adventurous Flute Concerto and a Romantically tinged Horn Concerto, one motif of which carries a pensive echo of the *Star Wars* title theme. Williams is devoted to the orchestra as an institution. He guest-conducts regularly at orchestras across America, often letting himself be used as a fund-raising tool. "Wherever you go, orchestras are playing better and better," he told me. "These institutions are at the core of artistic life in so many cities. I wish you would hear politicians bragging on that a little bit." Early in Williams's career, film composers received scant attention as creative figures. Now scholars like Lehman specialize in the field, and online fan sites chronicle minutiae. Williams is delighted by that attention, yet he wishes that concert composers also got their due. "I've heard a few pieces by a young American composer, Andrew Norman, who is very good," he said. "Might there not be a bigger audience for his work, too? I would love to see that." As it happens, the admiration is mutual: Norman has said that he first felt the pull of orchestral music while watching his family's VHS copy of *Star Wars*. If Williams looks at the contemporary-music world with a certain wistfulness, others have looked to him with kindred feelings. An unexpected friendship arose between him and the composer Milton Babbitt, who was long a leader of the diehard modernist camp in American composition, taking a combative stance toward neo-Romantic trends. In the years before Babbitt's death, in 2011, the two composers frequently wrote letters to each other. "How or why Milton had any interest in me whatever, I don't know," Williams said. "But I loved receiving his letters, in his tiny handwriting. He was very interested in Bernard Herrmann, and asked me questions about him. One time, I had written this little quartet, for the Messiaen combination of clarinet, violin, cello, and piano. Milton heard it because it was played at Obama's Inauguration. He rang me up and said, 'I liked the little thing you did.' He was on another plane of thought. I have a book of his where he talks about 'concatenations of aggregates.' But the funny thing is that he originally wanted to be a songwriter. He wanted to compose musicals. We both adored Jerome Kern, and often spoke of this. He famously said that he'd rather have written one tune by Jerome Kern than the rest of his oeuvre. That was the world I came out of, too, so we had lots to talk about." Toward the end of our conversation, Williams said, "I don't want to take up too much of your time." I took this to be a signal to wrap up, but I had to ask about a pattern that connoisseurs have noticed in his most recent *Star Wars* films: the timpani has an unusually prominent role in climactic scenes. In a memorable sequence in Rian Johnson's *The Last Jedi*, as Luke Skywalker confronts his latest nemesis, Kylo Ren, an obsessive four-note ostinato in the orchestra is banged out at full volume on the timpani—a ricocheting gesture that disrupts the blended orchestral texture. As it happens, these parts were played by Williams's brother Don, a veteran percussionist in Hollywood orchestras. I wondered whether there was any message hidden in this starring role for the Williams family instrument. Williams laughed and said, "Well, partly it's a practical issue. Because of the tremendous noise of the effects in these films, I have gone for a very bright trumpet-drum preponderance. But maybe there's some other element to it—I don't know. It has been an extraordinary journey with these films, and with my entire career as well. The idea of becoming a professional film composer, never mind writing nine *Star Wars* scores over forty years, was not a consciously sought-after goal. It simply happened. All of this, I have to say to you, has been the result of a beneficent randomness. Which often produces the best things in life."[4]

By Permission: Alex Ross, "The Force Is Still Strong with John Williams." *The New Yorker,* **July 20, 2020 (c) Alex Ross.**

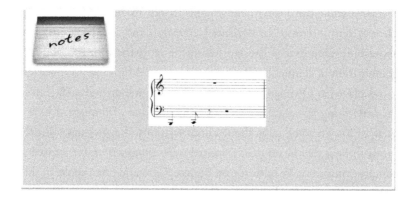

CHAPTER 3

THX (1983)

THX, the THX logo, and the THX Deep Note audio mark are registered trademarks of THX Ltd.

THX's Deep Note was created by Dr. James A. Moorer. His "The Deep Note" is THX's sound explosion.

> The sonic logo is used on trailers for THX-certified movie theaters, home video releases, video games, and in-car entertainment systems. The Deep Note debuted in 1983 at the premiere of Star Wars: Episode VI—Return of the Jedi in Los Angeles.[1]

The U.S. trademark registration for the first version of the THX sonic logo contains this description of it:

> *The THX logo theme consists of 30 voices over seven measures, starting in a narrow range, 200 to 400 Hz, and slowly diverting to preselected pitches encompassing three octaves. The 30 voices begin at pitches between 200 Hz and 400 Hz and arrive at pre-selected*

*pitches spanning three octaves by the fourth measure. The highest
pitch is slightly detuned while there are double the number of voices
of the lowest two pitches.*[2]

Dr. Moorer holds a PhD in Computer Science from Stanford University, granted in 1975. Prior to that, he earned an S.B. in Applied Mathematics from MIT in 1968, and an S.B. in Electrical Engineering from MIT in 1967. His website biography says

James A. Moorer is an internationally-known figure in digital audio and computer music, with over 40 technical publications and four patents to his credit. In 1991, he won the Audio Engineering Society Silver award for lifetime achievement. In 1996, he won an Emmy Award for Technical Achievement with his partners, Robert J. Doris and Mary C. Sauer for Sonic Solutions/NoNOISE for Noise Reduction on Television Broadcast Sound Tracks. In 1999, he won an Academy of Motion Picture Arts and Sciences Scientific and Engineering Award (Oscar) for his pioneering work in the design of digital signal processing and its application to audio editing for film. He is currently working at Adobe Systems, Inc. as Senior Computer Scientist in the DVD Team. From 1987 to 2001, Dr. Moorer has served as Senior Vice President for Advanced Development at Sonic Solutions, and is responsible for the NoNOISE package for restoration of vintage recordings. From 1986 to 1987, Dr. Moorer consulted for NeXT, Inc., on DSP software architecture for audio processing. From 1985 to 1986, he was the chief technical officer at the Lucasfilm Droid Works. From 1980 to 1985, he was the digital audio project leader at Lucasfilm, Ltd. From 1977-1980, he was the Reponsable Scientifique (technical advisor) at IRCAM in Paris. From 1975 to 1977, he was the co-director of the Stanford Computer Center for Research in Music and Acoustics. From 1968 to 1972, he was a professional programmer at the Stanford Artificial Intelligence Laboratory.[3]

Dr. Moorer told *Fast Company* in 2015 that the inspiration for the original Deep Note came to him in a flash. He imagined a sound that told an almost Biblical story about the creation of order from chaos, all in a single note. "That story of triumph over chaos is a fundamental human story, and I wanted to tap into it," he tells me by phone. "After all, what better way to signal the ultimate in audio quality than by trying to capture the voice of God?"[4]

Why does Dr. Moorer think we are still talking about Deep Note?

Well, it has legs and a persistence that I didn't imagine. I mean that's one of the things you shoot for of course, is to make something so gripping that people can't get it out of their head. Although it's funny because it's not something you can whistle exactly.[5]

Why does he think it's been so powerful? Could he have imagined sitting there that day creating this note that it would have transcended all these decades.

Well, I had a hint of it when I first started playing it around Lucasfilm because people would go out and call other people to come in and listen to it and they're a tough audience. So that was my first hint that this thing had some power to it. Well, plus I remember when I was first asked about it, you've heard this part of the story, but I'll say it again to make a point. He came up and said, I want something that comes out of nowhere and gets really, really big. And I thought I knew exactly what he wanted. And you know, from my musical studies and training, I knew what he wanted was a just tempered chord so that's what I built, that is a random cluster that converged. It builds up to this just tempered chord. I've had a number of comments that the chord seems bigger than life or bigger than normal or not like a chord that you would hear from an organ, even though that was sort of the idea. It was supposed to be sort of like a great big organ chord, but with a just tempered organ, which haven't been built in quite some time.[6]

Did George Lucas personally tell him to create it?

No, no, no, it was delegated. No, George has a policy of hiring from within or promoting from within. So when it came time to bring out the THX sound system, he wanted something to go in front of the film that announced that you're listening to a THX sound system. And so he delegated it to one of the up and coming sort of middle managers. He said if he threw him the idea and said, you make a 30 second logo to go in front of, it was Return of the Jedi in 1983, and as I say, he put together this lovely video, beautiful video animation, and he didn't say this, but I think what happened was that he spent all the money on the animation, didn't have any money left over for the audio and since I was on salaried staff there it didn't cost anything, so he went and pitched it to me. Lucas actually didn't hear it until quite a bit later. I've never asked George about it, but clearly it made an impression because they scrambled around to copyright it shortly after it came out.[7]

Did he intend for Deep Note to be one of the few sonic logos that you could hear and feel?

Yeah. That was sort of the intention. I mean, I was working closely with Tom Holman who designed the THX system and when you told me how many Watts he had behind the screen there, I thought, Oh boy, here's our big chance. Anything that can deliver that much power in a big theater, it'd be something like 3,500 Watts of audio and quite a bit of that in the subwoofer. So I figured, well boy, here's my chance to shake the rafters.[8]

So how does someone get from a PhD at Stanford and degrees at MIT into a studio creating sound logos?

Well, I've always been a musician and I've always been an engineer. I wasn't quite a good enough musician to make that a career. I did take a bunch of courses at our local music school at Florida State and Tallahassee, which is quite a large music school, but the number of unbelievable musicians that came through the place just couldn't convince me that, that I was in way over my head. So I got into MIT and thoroughly enjoyed it there. It was like a firehose of knowledge and information and the incredible, Emilio, all the professors around you have publication lists as long as your arm. And it was quite a few of them were very generous with their time and it was a wonderful environment, I learned quite a bit. After that I got a job as a professional programmer at Stanford. But the interesting thing there was that I worked at the Stanford artificial intelligence lab where there was a group of musicians that were professors at Stanford, composers that were using the computer to make music. I found this absolutely fascinating and helped out as much as I could and then I did get admitted to, after working there for about three years, I did get admitted to the graduate school in computer science there and I did a thesis with the music group there. In fact, it was a kind of a triple major, that is, computer science, electrical engineering, and music. That is my thesis committee consists of one EE prof, one computer science professor, and one music professor and it was on transcription of musical sound by computer. It is producing a score from a musical performance and boy using the computers of the day in 1975, that was a job. That was a serious job. I'm sure it would all be much easier now. From there within the music group, it was an incredible time because this was the early days of digital audio and just about anything we did was novel and was publishable and just about any funny noise you could make, you could write a paper on it and it would be something interesting, something that people wanted to read. So it was a wonderful time. As I say, everything we did turned to gold in a sense that is it helped composers make better pieces, it helped us understand hearing better. It was a glorious time. So I guess I had built up enough street creds by 1980 when George Lucas formed the computer division that I was the first name that popped up for the audio side of it. We had a nice little project running there for some years in digital solutions to film sound. And I never got a film credit, but I have sounds in a number of films like the asylum scene and Amadeus, some of them I did some of the noise reduction work there and a number of sound effects that Ben Burton, Gary Summers used in the Raiders of the Lost Ark movies. Some of which was based on some fairly elaborate signal processing, but not strictly musical in nature. But when I was throwing the ... I had indicated previously, as I mentioned, they had the policy of promoting from within. I'd mentioned previously that I did want to do some music for films. I wasn't quite ready to volunteer for a film score then, but any kind of music cue where I could do electronic music I would be up for, so this is the one that fell into my lap. So it's mostly for being in the right place at the right time and apparently with the right skillset.[9]

And when he's been in a theater and heard Deep Note, has he looked around to see anyone knows it's his creation?

Well, not only does nobody know it, it at various times other people have claimed it, which was also interesting. No, I don't make a big deal out of it, so, well, having said that, every time I give a big presentation, like a keynote presentation or something like that, I do play it first thing just to establish some identity.[10]

Why does he think some sonic logos like Deep Note are so powerful and so remembered for so few amount of time and notes?

Yeah, it's an interesting question. I honestly don't know. I mean, as far as Deep Note goes, I absolutely deliberately designed it to knock you flat. I mean, as soon as it was mentioned to me, I knew exactly what I wanted to do and I knew it would just stun everyone in the audience, at least the first time they heard it. And the others and the other composers, I don't know. I don't know what makes... Besides my obvious heavy handed approach to it. I don't know what makes some of these more subtle ones so attractive. A friend of mine [Mike Hawley] once said, where does the music happen? Is it in the musician? Is it in the score? Well, his conclusion was, no, it's in the listener. It's in the audience. That's where the music actually happens. So to explain why a piece has such attraction, you have to explain something about people I think and I'm not sure, quite, that I have any insight on that. He just passed away from cancer a few months ago. He was one of my hires at Lucasfilm. He worked with us for a couple of years and he worked at Next Incorporated and then he went to the MIT media lab, worked with Todd Machover, the composer among other people. But he was another one of these musical technical gadflies in the world. But, I thought that was a great quote.[11]

Does he have other favorite audio logos?

Yeah, I don't know about logos. There was an Apple commercial that came out a while ago that I absolutely adored. It was a three-note piano lick. Let's see if this is going to work. (Whistles). And then he made various counterpoints to it and built up a whole texture out of this three note motif. I thought that was absolutely brilliant.[12]

And when he hears his sonic logo now, what does he think? Is he still critiquing it?

Well, this last version that I did in 2014 I think I've taken that idea about as far as it can go. So I think I can say now that it is officially done. You know, I tried, I did have some fun playing with it, that is, I tried a longer versions of it where let's say the random lead up lasted, I had one version that was five minutes long and then I sat down at my keyboard and just, I retuned it to be the D natural on the piano keyboard. Normally it's a little bit high of a D and tried jamming to it, tried a little free jazz first and then try it a little boogie-woogie and that was sort of fun, but the piece as it is, stands on its own. In 2014 we did three different versions of it. A 30 second, a 45 second and a one minute. Of those I think the 45 second one is the best. The one minute one you start saying, get on with it. The 30 second one just doesn't build up quite long enough to convey the impact I wanted. Well, my use of space, the spatialization in 1983 was a bit impoverished. They only had four channels. Sound systems left center, right and surround, that is both left and right surrounds were for one channel. So it was nice to be able to do it in 7.1 and then the Dolby Atmos 9.1, which included two overheads. That was great fun. And then getting to use up to 80 voices. It's interesting because at some point adding more voices didn't help, it just made it sound if you have like 200 voices then it sounds like quite noise. It sounds like, you know, a storm outside or a vacuum cleaner or something like that. But 80 was about the limit and that one you could pick out individual voices every once in a while it would rise above the noise or would get an unusually high or unusually low or something like that and I thought that was a pleasant effect. I didn't want to lose that. The original was in 30 voices and I thought that was a little thin.[13]

And...finally, any funny reactions to Deep Note over the years?

Well, I did get the odd disturbing e-mail of there are some people that are absolutely terrified by it and that when they hear it coming on in the theater, they plug their ears up and bury their head in their lap until it's over. That wasn't exactly what I was going for. But, I can see how it might happen. Another one was very funny, which was that one of my friends commented that his dog went crazy every time the thing came on. There was one nasty little secret in the first one that, actually in the original, if you actually look at it on a spectrum analyzer of some kind, you'll see there's quite a bit of high-frequency material in there. And that's because to even get 30 voices, I had to cut some corners and it produced a bunch of high-frequency hash that is not really audible, but if you put it on an analyzer, it pops right up. And I think that's what the poor dog was hearing some stuff in the 15 to 18 kilohertz region.[14]

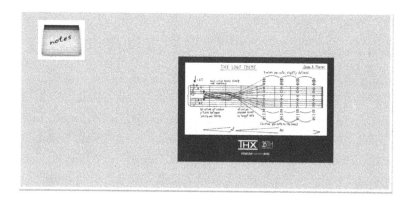

CHAPTER 4

Law and Order (1990)

Courtesy of NBCUNIVERSAL Media, LLC

It has stood the test of time. The sonic logo and the show. It was created by a Grammy award winner and he has gladly accepted his life with parole. Meet Mike Post. "The music for *Law & Order* was deliberately designed to be minimal to match the abbreviated style of the series. Post wrote the theme song using electric piano, guitar, and clarinet. In addition, scene changes were accompanied by a tone generated by Mike Post. He refers to the tone as 'The Clang.' The tone moves the viewer from

scene to scene, jumping forward in time with all the importance and immediacy of a judge's gavel which is what Post was aiming for when he created it. While reminiscent of a jail door slamming, it is actually an amalgamation of 'six or seven' sounds, including the sound made by 500 Japanese men walking across a hardwood floor. The sound has become so associated with the *Law & Order* brand that it was also carried over to other series of the franchise."

Mike Post (Leland Michael Postil) is a musician, composer, arranger and producer has long been considered the most successful composer in television history. Born and raised in Los Angeles County's San Fernando Valley, the son of an architect, Post began his study of music with piano lessons at the age of six. By fifteen, he was playing club dates. He graduated from Grant High School in 1962 with Mickey Dolenz of the Monkees and Magnum PI's Tom Selleck. He won his first Grammy Award at age 23 for Best Instrumental Arrangement on Mason Williams' "Classical Gas", a number 2 hit song in 1968. Post played for virtually everyone active in the LA recording scene during this time. Most notably he worked on all of Sonny and Cher's early hits, starting with I Got

You Babe. He formed The First Edition, featuring then unknown bassist/vocalist, Kenny Rogers. Post's debut as producer led to the group's Top Five single, I Just Dropped In (To See What Condition My Condition Was In). At 24, Post became Musical Director for The Andy Williams Show, becoming the youngest musician in TV history to hold such a position. Later, he returned to television as a producer for The Mac Davis Show. He also began designing stage shows—putting together acts for artists like Dolly Parton and Ronny Milsap. Post also produced Dolly Parton's hit album 9 to 5 and Odd Jobs in 1981. Much later, in 1997, he produced Van Halen's Van Halen III album. He's contributed arrangements to several Ray Charles LP's, produced, arranged and co-wrote (with Stephen Geyer) the Theme from The Greatest American Hero, which became a #1 record for singer Joey Scarbury. In 1981 Post hit the Top 10 again with his own recording of The Theme from Hill Street Blues, which featured guitarist Larry Carlton.

His career in television started in 1970. Over the years, he's written the music for seven thousand hours of TV including: *Law & Order: Special Victims Unit, Law & Order Criminal Intent, Law & Order, NYPD Blue, The Rockford Files, Magnum PI, Hill Street Blues, L.A. Law, The A-Team, Wiseguy, Hunter, The Commish, Quantum Leap, Doogie Howser MD, Blossom, Hooperman, The White Shadow, Hardcastle & McCormick, Byrds of Paradise, News Radio, Silk Stalkings*, and *Renegade*. Theme songs from *The Rockford Files, The Greatest American Hero, Hill Street Blues, and L.A. Law* all became chart topping records and landed Post four of his five Grammy Awards. In 1996 he won the Emmy for outstanding achievement in Main Title composition for the critically acclaimed *Murder One*.

This is the most successful sound in television history. It is, of course, the signature bleat from "Law & Order," something I surely did not need to tell you, which by itself is a measure of its greatness. Not a lot of shows employ this sort of aural calling card, perhaps because coming up with the perfect sound is not easy. Imagine invoking an entire television series and its themes with an audio flourish that lasts no more than a few seconds. Not a theme

song—that's a different matter, and far easier to create—just a
fleeting tone, honk, clang or other noise. The Hall of Fame for
such sounds would include the eerie four-tone introduction to
"The Twilight Zone"—distinctive and evocative, setting the stage
for weird, supernatural goings-on. And the ticking timepiece of
"60 Minutes"—an urgent, attention-must-be-paid sound perfect for a newsmagazine. And the shutter-click of "NCIS," with
its suggestion of "pause and examine closely"—the show's dominant law-enforcement tool. Towering over them all, though, is
the "Law & Order" dun-dun. Or chung-chung. Or bah-bonk.
Or DA-doink. Or however you want to describe it; everyone who
tries seems to do it differently. You'll know it if you hear it, which
is the very point: This two-beat metallic sort of thunk is instantly
recognizable all over the world, so much so that it has become an
object of parody. What makes it so right? Well, it helps that the
show that gave birth to it is one of the most successful series in
TV history, rerun and syndicated and spun off to the point that
the sound has been inescapable for 27 years. But mere ubiquity
doesn't crown you king of the TV mnemonics; you have to make
a statement, and the right statement. Or, in the case of this particular noise, several statements. It's the sound of a jail door shutting
and locking. Of a judge double-pumping to gavel a courtroom
to order. Of all the apprehensions and tensions of an urban night
condensed into the length of a heartbeat. Of a scripted TV show
with the gravity and aspirations of a well-made documentary. One
way to appreciate the brilliance of this or any of TV's other great
noises is to try to come up with a better one. Next time a "Law
& Order" episode flits across your television, mentally replace the
chunk-chunk with the sound of your doorbell, or car alarm, or
washing machine, or all three of those blended together. Not the
same, is it? Case closed.

What does Mike Post remember most about the audio logo?

Well, first off, let me work backwards. I had this friend Dick Wolf, who
had been a writer on a show that I did before *Law and Order*, called *Hill*

Street Blues. And he called me on a phone one day and he said, "Hey, I've got an idea for a show, would you have a drink and meet with me after work it is." Absolutely sure. I liked him as a guy, just a nice guy. So we sit down, and this is in the eighties and he says, "Our TV dramas about cops and doctors and lawyers and all the rest, they're not syndicating well. All syndication is really, really obsessed with half hours, like the *Cosby Show* and *Family Ties* and stuff like that." And I said, "Yeah, I'm aware of that, I am aware of." And then he says, "So I have this idea." And he said, "We'll shoot it as an hour show, but the first half hour will be the crime and the cops and the second half hour will be the lawyers and the prosecution and a trial." And I said, "Well, what are you saying? You're going to shoot it as an hour, but you're going to syndicate it in half hours." He goes, "Right." I went, "That's brilliant." I said, "What are you going to call it?" He said, "Law and Order." I said, "I'm in, count me in, please, please." And he goes, "Well I'm not sure what it's going to pay and you're the number one guy out there and just knowing you were interested, it'll help me in my sales job to the studio and then subsequently the network." So I said, "I don't care what you pay me, just let me in. Let me in, because this is a great idea." So he wrote a script; I loved this script. The studio and the network loved it and we shot it. And I did everything, I did the theme, the complete theme, which is a minute and some odd seconds long. And at the very last, I get a call from the dub stage when they're mixing all the dialogue and music and everything together. And it's Dick. And he goes, "Hey listen, I've decided that when we change scenes for most scenes, I'm going to date stamp it with a little, just say where we are and what the date is." And I said, "Okay." And he said, "I need a really distinctive sound for those scene changes." And I said, "Well, fantastic. Why don't you call sound effects since I don't do sound, I do music." And he goes, "No, no, no, no, please come on." I said, "I am not a sound effects guy, for God's sakes. I'm a composer, this is art." And he goes, "Archsmart, I need a sound. Give me a sound." So I said, "All right. All right." So I spent a day and a half sampling jail cell doors and clangs and I found a bunch of stuff that was weird. Like a bunch of men stomping on a floor, barefoot in Japan. It's like 200 guys stomping on the floor. And then I sampled some drums, I put it all together and I've got this chung, chung, ding, ding, chin, chin, whatever the hell you want to call it. And that's what you're referring to. So he's of course sent me a note, maybe five years, 10 years after *Law and Order*, the original was so successful and they'd made t-shirts with done, done or whatever on it and all the stuff. And he's send a note he simply said, "You've written a lot of great music in your life and won't you feel terrible that all you'll ever really be known for are two notes that aren't even music that are just a sound." I didn't laugh to, what the hell.

And what does he think of when he hears it now, after all these years?

I laugh, I laugh. I think the best testimony to it being effective as and to speak to how you've labeled it to, to be in a sonic logo. Once got a letter from a principal of a very large high school in, I think Cincinnati. Someplace in Ohio, Cleveland, or Cincinnati. And this lady said, "You've made my job so much easier." She said, "When I need a student to come to my office for disciplinary reasons." She goes, "I go on the Intercom, of course. And before I say his name or her name, I simply go ding, ding, or Chung, Chung." And then I say, "John Smith, please come to the principal's office." And she goes, "It strikes fear in the hearts of all of them." Hey, I thought that was really cool. I went, "Well, okay. That's some validation someplace that it did the job." And really and truly what Dick originally called me for I guess, and in your survey, with your students it would be true and in other words, can you make something that's so distinctive that when people hear it, they know exactly what it represents. So I guess that's successful. I think what happens as it applies to marketing, is that once you get a sound for something and the oral experience attaches to a visual experience and eventually is part of something that is emotional, so that people react to it. So at first they just reacted to the show, to the drama, to the acting, to the visual part of it and then you attach this to it and this feeds off of that. And then eventually that feeds off of this, right? Isn't that marketing thing now? About five weeks ago, my agent forwarded an email that came to their office from ESPN, from a radio producer at ESPN. And they said... This producer was so straight to the point. He goes, look, "We don't have anything to talk about on ESPN radio." He said, "We're dead in the water. We couldn't think of what competition we could create that would bracket with 64 like the March

Madness." So he said, "We came up with doing 64 greatest TV action adventure themes of all time." And so as we were putting it together he said, "It dawned on us that one guy had about 12 of them, so we thought we'd reach out and see if that guy would talk on the radio." And I called him right away and I said, "Listen, I'm actually a fan of both the people that are your hosts." And I said, "I actually listened to him in a car and I think that they're great and I'm a sports guy anyways." I said, "I'd love to do it." So I did three separate interviews over the ensuing weeks, while the public was voting on this. And it was bracketed, and I did have... I don't know, I had a bunch of them in there and I kept staying alive with one or more of them in the process of voting. And so it came down to the finals and I talked to them the night before their final voting. And it was the theme from Dukes of Hazzard against the theme from The A-Team. And I'd done The A-team and so they called me the next day with the great news that I had actually won this competition and I laughed my butt off.

What does he enjoy producing more: artists and themes?

I started out thinking I was going to be, a rock and roll record producer and an arranger. And I thought that that's where this whole thing was going to go because I had made it as a studio guitar player, young and I played on my first hip when I was nineteen which was, I Got You Babe by Sonny and Cher and I thought, "Well, I'm off to the races as a guitar player." And then I had ideas as an arranger. And then in order to protect the idea as this an arranger I became a record producer, so that a producer wasn't changing the ideas I was messing around with musically and blah, blah, blah. And then when my friend Steven Cannell, who had never sold a script. Started to get a little bit of traction as a writer in television, we were hanging out just as buddies and he kept saying, "I think your music would be great on TV. I think you'd be really good at this." And I'm going, "No, no, I'm in a rock and roll business. I don't need all this television baloney, I'm in a rock and roll focus." He finally got shows on the airwave he had the say as a producer and not just as a writer. And the minute I sat down to write music for a piece of film that didn't have any music with it I felt like, "I'm home. I mean this is where I belong, this is what I should be doing." There are basically two jobs there. The number one job is to create a theme that orally decides that identifies the show and relates to the show. So the first one anybody would know about that myself and my late partner Pete Carpenter did was the Rockford Files. But we also did all the music in the interior of the show called the score, the underscore Like Law and Order. I've done every note of Law and Order for 30 years. So I've yes, writing the themes is great and it's satisfying and it's fun to work closely with the producer and put into musical terms what he's saying in English words to me. And he's describing his hopes and his dreams for the project. It really is technically so much fun to take an entire 42 minutes of programming, 41 minutes of programming and put a music that makes a funnier parts funnier and the sadder part sadder and sexier part sexier and so on and so forth. I love in being part of enhancing drama or comedy to an audience, so that's really a fun job.

Not surprisingly, Post thinks television and movie music is pretty important.

So I'll give you a little hint that, so I'm from North Hollywood, California, right? And I still live in the same place and there's a buddy of mine that's 13 years older than me, it's from the same place. And we get together often and talk about this stuff. And his name is John Williams. And one example of, we've done a couple of dog and pony shows together because it's pretty funny. We're actually the exact same guy, he's professorial and legit not... But that's complete baloney. He's like me, he's just a musician, he's just happy to have a gig and happy to be working and tremendous sense of humor. Funny as hell. So at any rate, for this one thing that we did, they showed jaws. They showed some of the saints and jaws without music. And they were downright funny without music. They weren't scary at all. And then you put the music in there and everybody's going, "Holy moly, somebody's going to die here." So it's pretty funny and they did some of my stuff the same way and it is... You're 100% right. I don't know why music does what it does. It's magic, it really is magic going what it does for people's memories, for people's, for all the good parts of life and all the sad parts of life, I don't know. I've been doing it my whole life and technically I know everything there is to know about it technically. From an emotional standpoint I still, honestly I'm just feeling mystified by it and in awe of it. I don't know why, I know technically everything about it, I've been doing it my whole life. However, I can sit and play Bb/F to F and go, "God, why does that sound that way? Why does it affect me that way? Even after all these years, the simplest thing still affects me so strongly." People say, "God, you must be so proud." And pride is not the right word at all. I'm proud that I can work hard and I'm proud that I've never done anything that I couldn't look myself in a mirror about it. I'm proud that I've never been sued and I've never sued anybody. I've never felt cheated, and I know I've never cheated anyone and but pride is when you write something that you think is good, I'm honestly just the opposite. I get humbled by it and I'd go, "How in the hell did that happen?" And so your description, I will use that by the way. I just the guy that was standing there that got handed the notes and then somebody else is going to get added them next time, right?

So, Post is a big fan of John Williams, any others?

My God. I mean, come on friend. It's like Johnny is, he is just this Mount Everest of talent that... I mean, it's funny, the things that did I love are in one sense the most common things. I mean, if you could write a theme that's more... That means more and is just so automatic than Star Wars, I haven't heard it yet. I mean, now everybody says that, but I'm also the same way about... My wife and I were just flicking around and we happen to hit the natural, right at the home run sequence that Randy Newman did. And I mean, you cannot write a cue any better than that. I don't care how long you do this or how good you are or how... it's just perfect, it's absolutely perfect. And I mean, I was a big fan growing up of television and I was raised on a TV. Raised on a radio and raised on a TV. And so when I think back to my youth and the stuff that really moved me is like, I loved the theme from Lassie, I loved that thing. And then I met Nathan Scott who had written it and became friends with his son, Tom Scott the saxophone player. And then I loved the theme from Wild Wild West, I thought that was great. And then I got to work with Bob Conrad and be friends with him. I was a huge fan of *The Great Escape* the movie and then to get to work with Garner. And James Garner and do Rockford and all that. Just what a dream experience I've had to have all these idols. Ray

Charles, Chuck Berry, and not that Bach isn't an idol. I certainly never got to meet him, but I got to study his music. I'm all over the map, I'm one of those guys... There is no such thing as bad music, there's music that isn't performed really well or this or that, but I never heard any bad music. It's hard to screw it up to be honest with you. The really weird part of doing this for a living, whether you're doing it for commercials or you're doing it for big scores or you're doing it for symphonic music honesty guide, there's 12 of them. Okay. The 13th one's called an octave. So there were 12 notes in a chromatic scale. There are 12 different tones that make up a chromatic one ochre scale, right? The 13th one is a repeat of the first one. So just from a math standpoint, you've got to sit down and go, "Wait a second. This isn't quantum physics, this isn't molecular biology. This is finite, right? There's only 12 of these things. I mean, do the math. Come on." And then you dive into the deep hole that this all goes all the way to China, which is, "No, no. There's only 12 of them." And let's look at the ways that they can sound. Listen to the different things that can happen with those 12 bricks. You only got 12 bricks to make this wall and everything else is a repeat. So wouldn't you run out of colors? Wouldn't you run... Nope. Nope, how? It's so magical, it's so crazy. And then you think about everything that's happened in our lifetime, electronically and digitally and you see the possibilities and you go, "Wow." Then you go back and listen to Stravinsky or Orbach or anybody that lasted and you go, "How did these guys pull this off when the instruments that were made in those days weren't even in tune and more couldn't be played in tuning any effect." And you'll listen to that music and you go, "This is magic. This isn't from this earth. This is some other kind of something, this is crazy." I once had a really long conversation with Steven Bochco about, how many words are in a dictionary and how many notes are available in a scale. And we just laughed and laughed and laughed because we nerded ourselves into the next area going just thinking about creativity and then we compared it to painting and how many colors could you get. And then we painted it just we compared it to sculpture and it's just crazy nerdy stuff but very interesting and I've said a bunch of times to anybody that would listen to my nerdy stuff. And I think it goes back to the beginning of time, the beginning of man in the cave that all the really tough guys would go out and kill it. And then the strong guys would drag it back and the people that had the expertise will pull the skin off it and then the cookers would cook it, right? And while all that was happening, there were always a couple of weirdos over there drawing on the wall of the cave or there was one guy even before language was beaten on something and howl and all the civilians were over there and they looked over at the weirdos and went, "Who are these Martians? And why can't I do that? And why does it make me feel something?" Art and you go, "Yeah, it is, it is. If there's a God, that's how he speaks. He speaks in nature and he speaks in art and he speaks in emotionally, I think." I'm just lucky to have a life on it, to be able to do it and make a living from it.

And his favorite artists that he's worked with?

Unequivocally, Ray Charles just had idolized him since the first day I heard him. And then to get to meet him and then to find out that he liked my stuff too and that he wanted to me to do some arranging forum and hang with him, that was awesome. Between record production and composing for film television, I was Music Director of the Andy Williams Show for two years when I was 24. And then later the music director and the producer for the Mac Davis Show for a couple of years. And through that I got to work with the craziest assortment of really talented people from the opera singer Kathleen Battle to Dolly Parton to Ray, to Aretha, to Gladys Knight. All these just super, super talented people. So it's hard to say your favorite but if you had to have just one, I'd say Ray Charles. Yeah. He and I had this great conversation a couple of times of... His ears were just deadly. I mean, just absolute. I mean, things would squeak and he'd tell you what key it was in. But I said, "I think that your ears..." And he goes, "It's such baloney, because imagine how much I'd be able to digest if I could read music?" And he said, "Braille reading music takes so bloody long and you can't read braille music and play at the same time. You've got to read a couple of bars and then you play it. And then you read a few more bars." He goes, "He goes, nah." He said, "I think I'd be a much better piano player if I could read music." And I just knew it, okay whatever. On the other hand, there are people that you hear that are beyond talented. That are beyond almost beyond genius. Listen to Yo-Yo Ma and if you know anything about the cello you go, "Wait a minute, that's impossible. Nobody can do that. No, that's not possible on that instrument." And then there he is doing it and he can see and he's not... He hasn't had in quotes, a leg up of not being distracted by sight he could just zone in on what he's doing. It's a very difficult thing to figure out. And as you can tell, I've pondered all of this probably too much.

Any final thoughts from Post?

You'll never interview or speak to a luckier person than me. I've been making a living at music my whole life actually, since I was 16. I'm a shining example of if you do something that you loved and obsessed with and you'd be doing at night if they didn't pay you to do it during the day you never actually go to work, you just go to play.

CHAPTER 5

Intel (1994)

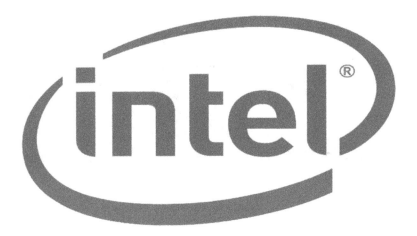

It is inside almost computer but most have never seen it.

It is played once every five minutes somewhere in the world.[1]

It took two weeks to create in a garage in Sherman Oaks, California.[2]

It is widely considered the best of the best.[3]

It has been called "the most famous three seconds of music in the world."[4]

He's called it "the mnemonic emperior."[5]

It's the Intel chip.

It's the Intel sonic logo.

And he ... is Walter Werzowa!

Walter Werzowa was born in Vienna, Austria, on December 15, 1960. He and his wife Evelyne currently reside in Los Angeles with their three children Camille, Julien, and Lucca. He studied classical guitar and

electronic music at Vienna Musik Hochschule where he collaborated with Otto M. Zykan on contemporary classical music.

Werzowa was in the band Edelweiss. It was an Austrian electronica/dance band consisting of remixers Martin Gletschermayer, Matthias Schweger, and Walter. The group is best known for their 1988 worldwide hit "Bring Me Edelweiss", and their European hit "Starship Edelweiss". Edelweiss reached the number one position with their hit "Bring Me Edelweiss," featuring Austrian folk singer Maria Mathis, who also did the live performances (and later recorded an updated version in 1999). The single was a hit in many European countries. Borrowing large parts of its melody from ABBA's "SOS" and Indeep's "Last Night a DJ Saved My Life", the song humorously targeted Austrian ski resorts and yodeling and sold five million copies worldwide.[6]

Werzowa shares a 'great story' about the ABBA sample:

When we decided to use the chorus of SOS in the Edelweiss song, we called the publishers in Sweden, the other publishers, and really this was pure luck. I guess I had so much luck in my life. A person picked up who obviously wasn't sober let's say it this way, and we basically conveyed at the time it wasn't unusual. Everybody took whatever they wanted to and sampling was just take it and use it in a song. This is like mid-1980s, and it was the Pioneer world of sampling and taking. We asked if we can implement the melody and write new lyrics. We asked for a fax verification of that yes. We got one of those faxes at the time, you know those things that your roll and they come out. Probably at this point, you won't even be able to read it anymore. Luckily, it got copied many times. That was it. We released it and it became a huge hit. It's always hoped for but not intended. And suddenly, we got this call from Sweden. The ABBA lawyers called and said basically, "Sue your up to the yin yang," because they thought we used it illegally. ABBA wanted to release a record at that time with a come back kind of idea. They said now that they destroyed the name they can't release it and all that, and damages, so still even though we knew that we had this paper we were a little bit scared, but that paper really helped. It was legally binding and I don't know what they did to that person who signed, but it all worked out fine.[7]

Werzowa immigrated the United States in 1991 after Edelweiss disbanded to complete a postgraduate program at USC for motion picture and television scoring. After an internship with Walt Disney Company writing music for movie trailers, Werzowa started his own company called Musikvergnuegen (German for "enjoyment of music.") The Intel project came from Kyle Cooper, a friend employed at the company R/GA in Los Angeles who had been hired by Dennis Carter, Intel's Chief Marketing Officer, to turn the Intel swirl into animation and sound. "Intel had a problem. A rapid development cycle meant microprocessor speed and capability were advancing quickly, but manufacturers weren't keeping up with the cutting edge. Manufacturers were reluctant to upgrade from the 286 chip to the 386, and consumers didn't know enough to care. "Intel's whole reason for existence was to push technology as fast as you can push it and then help the world adopt it so that everybody advances. And then do it again," recalls Carter. "1989 rolls around and we've introduced the 386 several years before. It's a very successful product, but it's not displacing the previous generation and that's a concern." Instead of continuing to market to manufacturers, the company decided on a new approach. In 1989, Carter led a pilot program in Denver that targeted consumers with a simple billboard campaign that became infamously known inside and outside Intel as the Red X campaign. It featured a crossed-out "286" with "386" written over it in graffiti. Before long, customers began asking for the 386 by name and manufacturers were forced to bake it into their products. The campaign was a success, but Intel would soon need a way to replicate the results on a much larger scale, and for a newer medium. After a court ruling stripped the naming trademarks for the 386 and 486, Carter looked for ways to evangelize Intel itself rather than specific processors. This would lead to the genesis of the Intel Inside campaign, launched in 1991 with the now-famous Intel swirl logo. Then in 1994, Intel was ready to expand to television, presenting a new set of challenges. "Nobody was going to run a 30-second ad with the logo there the whole time, it would look stupid. An audio component seemed like it would work really well," Carter said. "That audio component would become what might be the most iconic three seconds of branded audio ever recorded: The Intel bong sound."[8]

Werzowa says he didn't get much direction to compose the accompanying jingle. "The sound needed to convey reliability, innovation and trust," Werzowa said. He says the "Intel Inside" tagline triggered a melody in his head, and those were the notes that became the Intel bong sound: D flat, D flat, G flat, D flat, A flat. The rhythm of those four notes is patterned after the syllables in Intel's slogan: In-tel In-side. Werzowa spent weeks in his Sherman Oaks garage refining the five-note sequence into the jingle that's since become so recognizable. Each of the five tones is a blend of various synthesizers—mostly a lot of xylophone and marimba.[9]

"There're so many fond memories even around the production. It started in a very particular way that at the time Kyle Cooper, he was the junior designer at Imaginary Forces at the time, this was 93 I believe, called me and said he has this very different kind of job and I worked a lot with Imaginary Forces. He said, "You wouldn't believe somebody wants to have three seconds of music." Kyle and I were laughing on the phone and, "You have time to come in and I'll show you the boards?" He showed me the boards. There were six key frames of the Sonic logo in there and, and we were both a little bit frazzled. It's like, "Can you even write a piece of music which makes sense and it's three seconds long? You can't say a meaningful sentence in three seconds. Could you write three seconds of music?" I realized right away this is a very different kind of assignment. On my way back from the meeting in the car, I browsed and tried to get on my thoughts and in my head nothing really made sense. When I was back at my studio, I tried melodies playing the piano and the guitar and whatever. It was really, really difficult to make any sense with it. I had to present an idea on the coming Monday. The meeting was on a Thursday or Friday. It was like just a weekend. Two days in, I got really anxious and stressed with it and I put again the board on the piano and looked at it and suddenly I had that idea which now made history since the tagline was Intel inside and could read it and see it. Fortunately, nobody would say it, there wasn't any voiceover over the mnemonic. I thought if this was a song, I would try the melody Intel inside like the four notes. And then, I thought we're dealing with engineers so it needs to be something very straight and organized and a very clear pattern and since it had to be applicable to any culture, there are only a few intervals which really make sense in China as well as in India as well as in the United States and Austria and France and whatever. That's the fourth and the fifth which are very powerful. So basically constructed and didn't compose the mnemonic, and I think the rest is history. This was a very strong moment that moment when that idea came up, how to tackle it. And then later on, it was great to hear it every couple of minutes and it became the most performed melody in broadcast. For a composer, that's incredible. I have to admit, the first couple of month I wouldn't have dared to tell my Austrian music teachers that I've done this because before when I started music we had to write symphonies, which are at least 20, 25 minutes long. If I would've told any of my professors that I got a hit with three seconds, they would have laughed and dismissed it. Right now, when I talk to those teachers, they think, "Wow. This is a great accomplishment." At the time, I was really scared that they wouldn't acknowledge that as a big success. And then later on, when my kids heard that mnemonic on the radio, TV, it's like, "Oh, it's daddy's song." That was very great when your family is applauding and excited about it. Now even engineers when I talk to them they're like, "Oh, my God. You wrote that?" It is all around incredible to be behind that. Intel was always a fantastic company to work with and very encouraging. I'm really proud of it."[10] Werzowa says that it is "worth millions of dollars"[11] Even though he has declined to say what he earned for creating it, calling the amount "not really amazing.," he admits "if I would have kept the copyright [to the audio mark], I'd be a millionaire right now."[12]

Is it safe to assume he made more money off Bring Me Edelweiss off the Intel logo?

Honestly, I never added those things up. It's hard to say because Intel led into so many things and so did Edelweiss. It's hard to say. It's hard to quantify or qualify. Both were important. Probably the Intel story opened so many doors that probably there's more funds behind that than Edelweiss because I chose a career more in film and moving pictures and writing in that world than writing pop songs.[13]

Why does he think after all these years it has been so powerful of a sonic logo?

I think it changed over the years why it is so powerful. Right now, I do believe the strongest factor is attention span. Lately, the young generation caters best to six second video snippets, clips as advertisement, and the attention span is shorter and shorter and the media buy is extremely expensive. That's probably the second reason. Three seconds can be performed more often than a 30-second spot. It was definitely the first hugely media buy mnemonic out there and it really settled the land, so to say. From then on, people tried to copy it and every time something is copied, it made of course the original even stronger, so I think that's another reason. Yeah.

Intel gets supersonic credit for the fact that they figured out that they couldn't go to the consumer and say, "This is our chip and this is where it is and this is how much it costs and this is how it works." From a marketing perspective, they decided to go to companies and say, "Look, we've got this great logo, and if you put it in your commercials, we'll pay for a percentage of your advertising." Everybody will want Intel inside.

Werzowa agreed. You're absolutely right in what you're sharing. In addition to, for the three seconds at the end of God knows like Pioneer spots or whatever they were attached with, they not only said they would pay the media, but they would pay 25 percent actually in processes. If a company got that immediate buy help, they would get 25 percent in cash basically and the other 25 percent in processes. It was a win–win for all. I love those win–win situations where people come up with ideas that help everybody in the process. Yeah. As you said, nobody could touch the processors and nobody knew at the time really what it was unless you were a great engineer. Kyle and I looked at each other when we did the job and we knew that there are some things like those little centipedes in computers, but what a processor would actually do and why you would need them for us creatives it was nothing we would have had any idea about.

Others have agreed.
Fast Company said:

Forget the sound of the waves or the songs of birds, they didn't even make the top 10. But the jingle advertising a computer chip, and object which most of us have never even seen, took the prominent second spot in our brains in terms of addiction. We strongly respond to the sound of Intel! This tells us that repetition is the key, since most of us can't even sing it. What this tells us is that there's no limit to this phenomenon, because a computer chip doesn't really have a sound.

Forbes said:

Twenty-two years ago, three seconds of audio comprised of five musical notes was written to help a tech brand with its marketing. Today, you can't think of Intel without hearing the iconic "Intel Inside Bong." You've heard it so many times, even with different variations, but the core five note progression is always the same. How can something so simple be so effective? Well, when you really examine Intel's use of the mnemonic, you realize that it's hugely associated with its brand, and its success. What you hear are adjectives that the company wants you to associate with Intel: A modern, trustworthy, sleek, intelligent, simple and efficient brand. Yogiraj Graham, Director of Production for Intel Global Production Labs, explained, "The Intel bong is one of the most powerful assets we have. We're always looking for ways to showcase the amazing experiences that Intel enables, and the Intel bong sound helps keep our messaging consistent.

Since the original jingle premiered in 1994, Werzowa says he's updated it every two to three years. Now that the sound is globally recognizable, Intel is much more hands-on. The chipmaker's in-house creatives, marketing team and legal counsel all provide input before any changes can be made. It's hard to count how many versions the bong sound has gone through over 20 years, but while the visuals have changed and some bass has been added, the essential five-note sequence remains the same. Even william's brief tenure as Intel's director of creative innovation hasn't had much impact, although the Black Eyed Peas frontman sampled the jingle for his 2013 track "Geekin." Perhaps the most creative iteration so far is from a group of Intel engineers in Finland, who turned themselves into human cannonballs, and launched into a giant row of chimes—likely with the aid of some video-editing wizardry.[14]

In 2015, at Super Bowl 50, Intel released a new video called "Experience Amazing." It was a mash-up of images depicting Intel's presence in everyday life with the music from Beethoven's Fifth Symphony and an orchestral arrangement of Intel's familiar jingle-bong chime. For Werzowa, it marked a literal coming-home. The music for "Experience Amazing" was conducted and recorded with a 96-piece orchestra in an old music hall in Vienna, Austria. It's the city where Beethoven first premiered his Fifth Symphony, at the Theater an der Wien on December 22, 1808, and it happens to be the city where Werzowa was born and raised. It was thus of particular importance to Werzowa that the score be "done respectfully," he told Brief. "Growing up in Vienna, Beethoven was one of the heroes. He wrote [Symphony No.5] in Vienna, he lived in Vienna, he died in Vienna, and he's part of my culture and ancestry in that sense." Growing up and going to university in Vienna, Werzowa studied classical guitar and electronic music, but he also, crucially, studied architecture, which he attributes to sowing the seed of his ability to precisely pair visual and audio elements. "I think that's where it all started from," he said. "Music can tell stories and so can design or visual arts. If you look at, let's say, Moroccan carpet, it's information is a pattern which could be expressed mathematically, and if it's expressed mathematically you can translate it into music and vice-versa."[15]

How does someone go from Bring Me Edelweiss to Beethoven?

That's a good question. I'm a very curious person and I am workaholic and I love doing many different projects at the same time. I focus for two, three hours on one thing and then I love turning around and doing something else. In that sense, it's inspiring to work on this huge big symphony and at the same time with audio branding, at the same time sound design for something, and running the company in LA, and running a company here in Vienna and talking to different people. Every conversation is fruitful. It's like you and I talking inspires me to think more. I think this life is a great opportunity to learn and to grow.[16]

Werzowa has done more than the Intel logo. He has written music for other commercials and for more than two dozen movie trailers, including *Men in Black*, *The Crying Game*, *Addicted to Love*, *The Flintstones*, and the recent remake of *Psycho*. He scored the documentary, *Author: The JT LeRoy Story*, which was written and directed by Jeff Feuerzeig and is the only film on this subject thus far to receive American and European theatrical distribution, it premiered in United States theaters in September 2016. He scored the main themes to *Eraser* (starring Arnold Schwarzenegger); *Taking Lives* (starring Angelina Jolie); *The Hunted*; *Yippee and The Devil;* and *Daniel Johnston*, which received a Sundance Film Festival award. He also earned a music credit on Steven Spielberg's *Minority Report* and in 2008 he worked on *8: Person to Person*, which was directed by Wim Wenders. He also composed the Nova theme. In 2014, Music Beyond, the production music library founded by Werzowa in 2005, was acquired by BMG. He now serves in a consultant capacity at both BMG and Beyond. In 2016, Werzowa launched HealthTunes.org, a free music/sound streaming platform that offers academically and scientifically researched Health Music and evidence-based clinical reference.

But, if his legacy is the Intel sonic logo, is he ok with it?

Luckily, it's short enough so it would fit on a tombstone. You can write those four notes up there and then people might even know them and can sing them when they see them. Yeah. That might be a great idea. I'm really proud of it, and most of it because Intel really inspired my thinking in terms of innovation and becoming a tech nerd in a sense. It's like I love music, music is my passion and creating sound, but with Intel I think more of my drive to know about technology. Over the years, that helped with many projects and museum projects and coming up with ideas, really creative new ideas. Right now, I'm doing this project which would not fit on my tombstone, but I'm really proud of. I'm writing with Ahmed Elgammal. He's this AI professor genius at Rutgers University, the 10th symphony, Beethoven's 10th symphony. That's an incredible opportunity. In a sense, that was also my life with Intel is leading me to that because they've done so many great projects over the years where technology was important, and doing this now with AI and machine learning and all of that, Intel really helped that journey as well. And now writing with Beethoven and AI, the 10th symphony, is something extremely meaningful.[17]

Next to his, what is Werzowa's favorite sonic logo?

I have to say T-Mobile is definitely really, really up there. It is so simple, so memorable and it's so difficult to be simple and not stupid. It's just so easy those days just to play quickly in three seconds some notes, but it doesn't make much sense. T-Mobile really hones into the logo. It basically scores the visual of the logo with the dots. That's really brilliant and very powerful as well. I'm so honored that we work with Lance Massey who composed that. He's a great guy and a wonderful thinker as well as somebody who doesn't just write, compose and that's it. He thinks about it and has stories, why, what is meaningful in his audio brandings.[18]

Does Werzowa have any final thoughts on sonic logos and their future in branding and advertising?

I think they have to become better and trickier. It's not just a melody. I want to encourage the composers and the agencies, the advertising agencies and the corporations themselves to really think about what the product and the philosophy is standing for, and think of new ways how to propel that. We have so many possibilities now. We can do so many things and can be so innovative that it's not just a three second melody or two second melody anymore. It is so much more. I had this interview with Stewart Copeland, the drummer of *The Police*, and he invited me because of Intel and we jammed around a little bit and fooled around a little bit. He's just such a brilliant musician and said, "What could be a next logo and what could we do?" We basically jammed around for probably half an hour. I had a couple of fun ideas, but again it has to fit for the company and you have to study the company when you write for a corporation, really know everything, know about the product as well as the leadership to make it fly.[19]

And final thoughts from Werzowa on his success?

Definitely I got lucky and then I learned a lot. Maybe that's what Austria told me, to be spontaneous and always make the best of it. It's just every day learning more.[20] And he's a Jeopardy question!

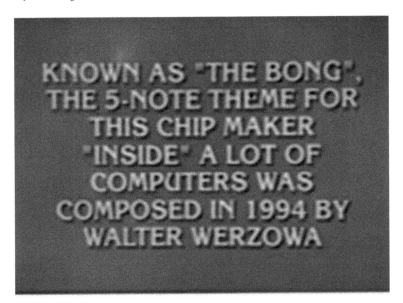

KNOWN AS "THE BONG", THE 5-NOTE THEME FOR THIS CHIP MAKER "INSIDE" A LOT OF COMPUTERS WAS COMPOSED IN 1994 BY WALTER WERZOWA

Note: Intel is the sole owner of all rights to the Intel audio and visual logo. Intel's significant investment in the use, promotion and licensing of this mark has elevated it to the status of a strong sound mark, one of the most significant sound marks of all time. Based on Intel's use (making sure that consumers understand that when they hear these five notes that they are getting Intel's goods and services), Intel has been able to successfully register this sound in trademark offices around the world (often being the first registered sound mark in many of these jurisdictions).

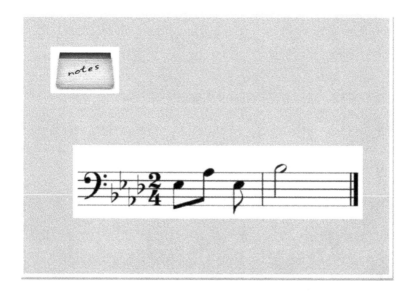

CHAPTER 6

Windows (1995)

Courtesy of Microsoft

It came from a man who later admitted he had never used a PC.

It took him less time to create it than the time it takes to boot up a PC.

He is Brian Eno.

It is the Windows 95 sonic logo.

Born on May 15, 1948, in Woodbridge, Suffolk, he was christened Brian Peter George Eno. His father, William, was a postman, and his mother, Maria Buslot, who was Flemish, stayed home. When Eno was eleven, he entered St. Joseph's College, a Catholic grammar school in Ipswich. According to *On Some Faraway Beach*, David Sheppard's excellent biography, the school encouraged students to incorporate some part of the school's religious heritage into their identities, so Eno called himself Brian Peter George Jean-Baptiste de La Salle Eno, after the patron saint of teachers. Eno has long had a vaguely aristocratic bearing, implacable and seemingly above the fray, which makes it seem plausible that he came from a long line of European clerics. People often refer to Eno now as a boffin, or describe him as looking like a professor or an architect. When I met him, in 2013, he was wearing a variety of comfortable fabrics that I couldn't identify. He looked like someone who owns lots of expensive things, which he does, and is used to being listened to, which he is. After St. Joseph's, Eno attended the Ipswich Art School, beginning in 1964, and then moved on to the Winchester School of Art, in 1966. At Ipswich, he studied under the unorthodox artist and theorist Roy Ascott, who taught him the power of what Ascott called "process not product." Having never mastered an instrument, Eno began experimenting with tape recorders, at the urging of an instructor and friend named Tom Phillips, who introduced him to the work of John Cage and the Fluxus group. At Winchester, Eno performed "Drip Event," by the Fluxus member George Brecht. The entire "score" of "Drip Event" reads: "Erect containers such that water from other containers drips into them." Eno then wrote a piece whose instructions read: The instruments are in turn ground down and individually cast into blocks of acrylic resin. The blocks are given to young children. Though Eno drew and painted at both Ipswich and Winchester, he left school with no plans to become a fine artist. "I thought that art schools should just be places where you thought about creative behavior, whereas they thought an art school was a place where you made painters," he said later: "I think negative ambition is a big part of what motivates artists," Eno told me. "It's the thing you're pushing against. When I was a kid, my negative ambition was that I didn't want to get a job." After leaving Winchester, in 1969, Eno moved to London and became involved with a sprawling group called the Scratch Orchestra, led by the composer Cornelius Cardew. The orchestra conducted various "happenings," some of which involved promenading through public spaces while playing, almost all of its work emphasized improvisation over technical skill. In 1970, Eno ran into the saxophonist Andy Mackay, a friend he'd met while at Winchester. "Have you still got some tape recorders?" Eno recalls Mackay asking him. "I'm in this band, and we need to get some proper demos made." Mackay owned a small synthesizer, operated with a joystick and small pinboard, which he encouraged Eno to take home and experiment with—a moment in pop history that is roughly equivalent to Jimi Hendrix's discovering feedback. Eno mastered the instrument by using it as something other than an instrument. He fed the band's music into the synthesizer, then sent the processed result through various tape decks and out through a P.A. system whose elements he'd collected over the years.

The band began rehearsing in Eno's house, with Eno acting as "sound manipulator," a cross between a live-sound engineer and a band member. The outfit's leader, Bryan Ferry, eventually chose the name Roxy Music. By the end of 1972, the band was famous in the United Kingdom, no member more so than the partly bald man with his long hair painted silver. Eno started his live career with Roxy Music by setting up at the back of the venue and ended up onstage, sometimes playing his synthesizer with an oversized plastic knife and fork. Tired of butting heads with Ferry, Eno left the band in 1973, after two albums. It was his last stint as a permanent member of a touring act. But he was still under contract with Island Records, which had faith that Eno could become his own kind of pop star. In 1974, with various musician friends he'd collected over the years, he released two albums, "Here Come the Warm Jets" and "Taking Tiger Mountain (By Strategy)." The first album yielded a minor hit, "Baby's on Fire," written on the day Eno walked out of a meeting with Roxy Music, burdened with debt but so happy to be out of the band that he felt like jumping in the air. Both albums are perverse, slightly agitated, and playful, with many of the lyrics generated randomly and cut together from various sources (mostly Eno's own notebooks). Eno began "Another Green World" (1975), his third solo release and a gentle masterpiece, without having written any material. By prodding a group of musicians to improvise and then editing that material, he created something consistent and coherent. The album is stubbornly placid: distorted guitars heat without burning, bass lines circle without begging for change, and drums are placed so as to suggest upward growth more than forward motion. It is a very hard album to wear out. There is also a fair amount of singing, which somehow you forget every time you look at the album cover. The record fulfills the implied promise of the title, making the trace of a human voice surprising every time. Reflecting on the work, Eno said, "Someone told me that he read an interview with Prince, where Prince said that the record which most influenced him was my 'Another Green World,' which was incredibly flattering. It's my understanding that Prince had picked up on the idea that you could have records that were kind of sonic landscapes with vocals on them, and that's sort of what 'Another Green World' was." For most of his career, Eno has stuck to manipulating synthesizers or tape, give or take a digital innovation, and is credited on many albums as providing "treatments." But he has taught himself most of the standard rock instruments, and sings on most of his own recordings. (For many years, he has been holding a weekly chorus of nonprofessional singers in London.) The credits for "Another Green World" make it clear that Eno was almost as interested in changing the language of rock as he was in saying anything specific. He is listed as playing several previously unknown varieties of guitar: "castanet," "club," "desert," "digital," and "snake," in alphabetical order. His careful but violent processing makes these names more accurate than you'd expect. In fact, Eno had already described the "snake guitar" to NME's Ian MacDonald two years earlier: " 'Snake guitar' requires no particular skill . . . and essentially involves destroying the pitch element of the instrument in order to produce wedges of sound that can be used percussively or as a kind of punctuation." Use noninstruments. The pairing of "In Dark Trees" and "The Big Ship" on side one of the LP presents Eno's developing blend of odd and peaceful. The music is unobtrusive and instrumental: the first track is two and a half minutes, the next one barely three. "In Dark Trees" feeds a primitive rhythm generator (it was not yet called a drum machine) through the synthesizer, producing a tannic stutter. One guitar voices small unresolved chords that chatter through yet more echo. A second guitar enters after a minute and plays a slow minor-key figure that slides down the neck. It repeats three times, fading out on the fourth round. "The Big Ship" is anchored by a synthesizer playing unceasing sustained chords that suggest a hymn. (Hymns have been an obsession of Eno's since childhood.) A guitar rises up in a distorted swell, following the chords closely, playing the root note of each one. The chords cycle without changing, though a contrapuntal arpeggio sneaks in and plays against the chords as they fade. The two songs quickly sketch two different spaces, one moist and shrouded, the other warm and open. By ignoring the virtuosic, personality-led rumble that his former bandmates in Roxy Music were making, Eno was moving toward a music that changed your perception of the space around you. Geography could be as memorable as melody. Eno's strategies don't always appeal to the musicians he works with. In Geeta Dayal's book about the album, also titled *Another Green World*, the bassist Percy Jones recalls, "There was this one time when he gave everybody a piece of paper, and he said write down 1 to 100 or something like that, and then he gave us notes to play against specific numbers." Phil Collins, who played drums on the album, reacted to these instructions by throwing beer cans across the room. "I think we got up to about 24 and then we gave up and did something else," Jones said. In 1972, not yet a producer, Eno made his first visit to New York. He told *Disc* magazine that he already felt "emotionally based" in the city. In 1978, Eno returned to New York, ostensibly for a short stay, but remained until 1984. He said that "one of the most exciting months of the decade . . . in terms of music" occurred in the summer of 1978. "No!" Through friends, Eno heard about No Wave, then the dominant style for downtown bands who were taking punk to its logical extremes—abandoning song form, playing entirely outside of formal tunings, and foregrounding noise over signal. For the compilation "No New York," which Eno produced for Antilles Records, he picked a number of bands to represent the scene. Teenage Jesus and the Jerks, Mars, DNA, and the Contortions were included on the album, a fair slice of the smartest and most aggressive bands of the time. The album became famous, years later, as a reflection of a moment, but it is also valuable because many No Wave bands recorded so little during their brief careers. These four bands, however, did make recordings, which are all truer to their spirit than Eno's vision of them. They all exhibited a faith in dissonance, distortion, or confrontation—sometimes all at once. The "no" in No Wave was important, and Eno, as sharp as he was to recognize the scene, still operated with a spirit based on the continuous Yes. "No New York" disoriented and teased where it needed to punch and bite. Right around the release of "No New York," Eno produced "Q: Are We Not Men? A: We Are Devo!," the début by Devo, the visionary band from Ohio. Producing DNA, Devo, and Talking Heads in the same year shows impeccable taste. But taste is not an act—it's an opinion. On the astonishing, criminally out-of-print "Devo Live: The Mongoloid Years," you can hear Devo performing at Max's Kansas City in 1977. Even in low fidelity, their rendition of "Uncontrollable Urge" is merciless, an inhuman sound that summons a human reaction. Few bands have had a similar combination of hostility and control. Under Eno's watch, "Uncontrollable Urge" became slower and tranquillized—it moved with an unnecessarily light swing. Devo's Jerry Casale told the Guardian, in 2009, that the band found Eno's approach "wanky." "We were into brute, nasty realism and industrial-strength sounds and beats," Casale said. "We didn't want pretty. Brian was trying to add beauty to our music." What became increasingly clear in the seventies was that Eno's embrace of possibility and chance wasn't as free-form as it seemed—it was a specific aesthetic. His name shows up on very few records you would describe as hard or aggressive, and his love of the perverse has never been rooted in hostility. Eno fights against received wisdom and habit, but rarely against the listener. In fact, as Eno found more ways for technology to carry out his beloved generative rules, his music became less and less like rock music and closer to a soundtrack for meditation. The same year that he released "Another Green World," he also put out "Discreet Music." The A side was a thirty-minute piece that was written as much by machines as by Eno. In the liner notes, Eno wrote, "If there is any score for the piece, it must be the operational diagram of the particular apparatus I used for its production. . . . Having set up this apparatus, my degree of participation in what it subsequently did was limited to (a) providing an input (in this case, two simple and mutually compatible melodic lines of different duration stored on a digital recall system) and (b) occasionally altering the timbre of the synthesizer's output by means of a graphic equalizer." The result is an area of sound without borders or time signature. There is no rhythm track, just layers of monody, lines programmed into a synthesizer and playing over each other. It is hypnotic, and fights your attempts to focus on it. In 1978, he started to use the term "ambient music": the concept stretched back to describe "Discreet Music" and the work of earlier composers, like Satie, who coined the term "furniture music," for compositions that would be more functional than expressive. In the liner notes of "Ambient 1: Music for Airports" (1978), Eno wrote, "Ambient Music must be able to accommodate many levels of listening attention without enforcing one in particular; it must be as ignorable as it is interesting." But "Music for Airports" was not nearly as docile as Eno wanted it to be. Though the music is gentle enough to be background music, it is too vocal in character and too melodic to be forgotten that easily. I can recall entire sequences without much difficulty. As much as Eno wanted his music to recede, and as potent as the idea was, he failed by succeeding: the album is too beautiful to ignore. But, in some ways, history and technology have accomplished what Eno did not. With the disappearance of the central home stereo, and the rise of earbuds, MP3s, and the mobile, around-the-clock work cycle, music is now used, more often than not, as background music. Aggressive music can now be as forgettable as ambient music. In May, 2013, Eno gave a talk at the Red Bull Music Academy, in New York. Interviewed by the journalist Emma Warren, Eno said that he had created music for a hospital in Brighton, most of it not commercially available. We heard a snippet—it was Eno music, for sure, with muffled bell tones and sustained notes that avoided either high or low extremes in pitch. As much as this may be a default sound for Eno, he sees his music as addressing the parasympathetic part of the nervous system, which, he said, "deals with digest and rest, and calm down and connect things together, and so on." It was as if Eno had been drawn to a set of sounds that he has spent his life working with, only to find out later why he chose them. Eno told me that he heard from a fan who manages a supermarket in London and decided to play "Discreet Music" there. A week later, Eno went to visit him. "He said, 'It was lovely—people stayed much longer in the shop and bought far less.' I thought that was a very nice thing to say about the music." The most successfully ambient of Eno's ambient albums is the 2012 release "Lux." The core of the piece is twelve patterns, which use only the notes corresponding to the white keys on a keyboard. Eno brought an early version of the piece to a gallery in the Palace of Venaria, near Turin. He said that the gallery, a long space connecting two wings, is "all stone and glass, so it's very echoey." The first version of the piece didn't work in the space, so Eno began reworking it. He used the "convolution reverb" feature of the popular music-programming software Logic Pro. It allows you to record a sound—like a handclap—in a space, and then produce a simulation of that space's natural resonance. In the privacy of his London studio, Eno could play sounds "in" the Venaria gallery. He found a certain register, between three and five kilohertz, that "really seemed to sing in that space," and directed the piece toward that range. The musician Leo Abrahams played a guitar-synthesizer hybrid, and the violinist Nell Catchpole played along to the original patterns. "The process of making the skeleton of it was generative, in the sense that I set in motion various processes and let them do their thing," Eno told me. "But what was different this time was I thought, O.K., I'm going to listen to that, and I'm going to find out where the sort of moments are that something unusual happens, some-thing you didn't expect happens, and I'm going to work on them—so from a generative beginning I then went into composer mode, basically, which I haven't ever done before. In the past, I've really let the thing just carry on, do its thing." The result is both remarkable and almost impossi-ble to remember. I've listened to "Lux" as often as any of Eno's work, but I don't think I could reproduce five sequential seconds, even by hum-ming. I just know it. Eno has two new albums made in collaboration with Karl Hyde, "High Life" and its companion, "Someday World," released in May. "Someday World" uses unfinished pieces from the early nineties that Eno described as "polyrhythmic musical textures." Hyde played gui-tar over these tracks and contributed most of the lyrics, which are stripped of ego in an appropriately Eno-like fashion: many began with phrases Hyde heard spoken on the streets. One of the album's shortcomings is its thin sounds. This is odd, as Eno is typically adept at processing sounds until they are pleasantly far in timbre from their source. The horns embed-ded in "The Satellites" and "Daddy's Car" blat feebly, recalling a dog toy underfoot. The few pleasures on "Someday World" are Hyde's plainspo-ken but unpredictable lyrics, his stringent guitar playing, and the woody thrum of Eno's multitracked voice. (Hyde provides the album's main vocals.) "Who Rings the Bells" is the song to keep. Two guitars chip out interlocking patterns over a simple, active beat. Hyde's vocal phrases are long and relaxed, occasionally sung with another voice in harmony. "Who rings the bells? Who pulls the rope? Who barks like a dog?" He sings these words with the same languor Eno exhibited on his solo albums of the seventies, as if pitches were both easy to hit and not that important. Finally, though, "Someday World" is, at best, a good advertisement for Hyde as a singer and guitar player and a terrible introduction to Eno. Much better is "High Life," recorded in April, after "Someday World." Wanting to extend their work together, Eno and Hyde decided to record in front of several journalists. With typical Eno perversity, this surprise appendix easily outstrips the main text. Eno and Hyde sound energized and make forty-five minutes—the same length as "Someday World"—fly by. "Return" is built from Hyde playing his guitar with what sounds like a drumstick, making a clacking eighth-note ostinato that almost rings a chord while also muting it. Several layers of this guitar playing build up a pleasantly shifting rhythmic center, like Steve Reich's moiré patterns. Hyde sings out loud in harmony, and the whole song rises imperceptibly, forcefully, and then ends, nine minutes feeling like four. "DBF" is an instrumental derived from the same ideas undergirding the earlier Eno productions "My Life in the Bush of Ghosts" and "Remain in Light"— the clipped guitar sounds and drumming architecture of Afrobeat tricked out with, as the album credits put it, "slicing and treatments." It's alive and fluid, as comfortable and sure of itself as "Someday World" is past its sell-by date. The best sonic collision is "High Life"'s third track, "Time to Waste It," which pairs voices with a reggae rhythm, quiet and driven only by a trace of percussion. The dangers of British people futzing around with reggae—a clear and present menace, now and forever—are deftly avoided by making everything on the track (except for guitar upstrokes) sound like anything but reggae. Hyde's processed voice is eerily like Dolly Parton's, even when it's massed up high in digital reverb. This is Eno's comfort zone—elements you've heard before, turned over and laid across each other at funny angles, rejecting the standard order yet admitting pleasure. In 1980, Eno produced the Talking Heads' "Once in a Life-time," one of the songs that I manage to remain intimidated by no matter how often I play it. Like most of "Remain in Light," the album on which it appears, the track is heavily indebted to the Afrobeat of Fela Kuti, the influential Nigerian bandleader whose music Eno introduced to David Byrne. Eno's production of this transparent, polyrhythmic light box, it turns out, is based on a mistake—his own. "That song was a very good case of people not agreeing about the one," he told me, referring to the first beat of each measure. "I always heard it in a different place from everyone else, so I just kept sort of building things onto my one." Eno's haphazard instinct helped turn the brittle and wary Talking Heads into a supple, playful, Dada-esque dance band. Eno often works with highly skilled musicians, and then asks them to play against their own virtuosity. In this, he reminds me of Matisse, whose late work is his least ponderous: the scissor cuts of paper, often in leaflike shapes, are also a sort of rule-based art. He could no longer paint, so the method had to fit his body. And it was better. The scissors determined the aesthetic as much as his brain did. "I have a trick that I used in my studio, because I have these twenty-eight-hundred-odd pieces of unreleased music, and I have them all stored in iTunes," Eno said during his talk at Red Bull. "When I'm cleaning up the studio, which I do quite often—and it's quite a big studio—I just have it playing on random shuffle. And so, suddenly, I hear something and often I can't even remember doing it. Or I have a very vague memory of it, because a lot of these pieces, they're just something I started at half past eight one evening and then finished at quarter past ten, gave some kind of funny name to that doesn't describe anything, and then completely forgot about, and then, years later, on the random shuffle, this thing comes up, and I think, Wow, I didn't hear it when I was doing it. And I think that often happens—we don't actually hear what we're doing. . . . I often find pieces and I think, This is genius. Which me did that? Who was the me that did that?"[1]

How did you come to compose "The Microsoft Sound"?

The idea came up at the time when I was completely bereft of ideas. I'd been working on my own music for a while and was quite lost, actually. And I really appreciated someone coming along and saying, "Here's a specific problem—solve it." The thing from the agency said, "We want a piece of music that is inspiring, universal, blah- blah, da-da-da, optimistic, futuristic, sentimental, emotional," this whole list of adjectives, and then at the bottom it said "and it must be 3 1/4 seconds long." I thought this was so funny and an amazing thought to actually try to make a little piece of music. It's like making a tiny little jewel. In fact, I made 84 pieces. I got completely into this world of tiny, tiny little pieces of music. I was so sensitive to microseconds at the end of this that it really broke a logjam in my own work. Then when I'd finished that and I went back to working with pieces that were like three minutes long, it seemed like oceans of time.[2]

Ironically, Eno used a Mac to create the piece, admitting to BBC Radio 4 in 2009 that "I've never used a PC in my life; I don't like them."[3]

"Brian Eno is often credited with the invention of ambient music."[4]

In January this year I had an accident. I was not seriously hurt, but I was confined to bed in a stiff and static position. My friend Judy Nylon visited me and brought me a record of 18th century harp music. After she had gone, and with some considerable difficulty,

I put on the record. Having laid down, I realized that the amplifier was set at an extremely low level, and that one channel of the stereo had failed completely. Since I hadn't the energy to get up and improve matters, the record played on almost inaudibly. This presented what was for me a new way of hearing music - as part of the ambience of the environment just as the colour of the light and the sound of the rain were parts of that ambience.[5]

It started on a low note that ascended glissando-like by the fourth and then jumped up an octave to four identical high notes—a static 'melody' that remained open, unresolved. Under the four high notes a synthesizer drone increased in loudness, ending abruptly. The heraldic function is therefore realized by the same attributes as the Majestic Fanfare—a steep rise up and an unresolved ending. But the timbre is quite different. No trumpets here, but a soft, chime-like sound, suggesting a calm, new age mood (the tune was composed in the 1990s), as if sitting on a verandah, listening to the tinkling of a chime and contemplating the blue sky. Yet there is also an electronic edge, suggesting technological perfection. And unlike the Majestic Fanfare, no sense of group identity is invoked, reminiscent of television commercials from the period which showed people working with laptops in remote locations, amidst the grandeur of nature, with no human being in sight.[6]

By permission: "Ambient Genius," Sasha Frere-Jones, *The New Yorker*, June 30, 2014. Sasha Frere-Jones, *The New Yorker* © Conde Nast.

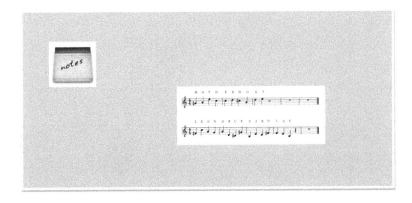

CHAPTER 7

T-Mobile (1990)

·T·Mobile™

The T-MOBILE and T trademarks, and the T-MOBILE music jingle, are regis-
tered trademarks owned by Deutsche Telekom AG, and are used with permission.
It plays more times than your phone rings.

He was Maxim.

It's the T-Mobile sonic logo.

And on the line is Lance Massey.

"It's the 'ding-a-ling-a-ling' tune, identified with T-Mobile for many
years, written by Lance Massey, founder of NeuroPop, an aural therapy
business that develops "health and wellness" products in audio form. The
winner of a global competition, it was based upon the T-Mobile logo
featuring gray dots and a pink letter T. "I used one of the NeuroPop algorithms to assign a middle C to a dot, and the pink T got the major third
above it," says Lance. How long did it take him? "I had years of research
and training to know what to do when the time came," he says, "but
when the time came, it took me about 15 seconds."[1]

Massey's LinkedIn page says:

I'm not normal. Yes, I can architect and develop software, web,
and mobile applications from concept to deployment, and I can
create custom music for global brands and media. This has honed
my perspective on company challenges and leads to unique, efficient, cost effective, and highly creative solutions. After over a
decade of experience launching everything from Flash scripts to

webapps used by millions of people I can now apply that perspective across multiple domains—tech, business, product, branding, strategy, etc. As CTO of The Limbic Group, I've architected and built SMS, iOS, and Android apps with React Native, socket-io, node/express, MongoDB. Fun fact: During my tenure in the New York music scene, I wrote the T-Mobile ringtone, making me more played than the Beatles.[2]

So how did "a little redneck kid in Tennessee"[3] come to write one of the most famous sonic logos?

I was studying under Gary Nelson at Oberlin Conservatory, and he got me interested in synthesizers, algorithmic composition, those sorts of things. Then I went on to become a commercial writer way back in the eighties, and I just carried all of that information with me. So basically, I wrote commercials for almost 15 years. Then after doing the T-Mobile logo, I retired because I thought I was going to make a ton of money, which ended up sadly being false. So when the money ran out, I switched to being a programmer and a tech entrepreneur. Which is probably why you can't find any information on me anymore, because I technically dropped out of the music business almost 20 years ago, and only recently started getting my production chops back up again to see if I could have a second go at it.[4]

What does he remember about the creation of the now famous T-Mobile sonic logo?

So it's one of those things where it literally took me less than 15 seconds to come up with it, but it was the 15 years of experience before that led to it. Again, the algorithmic composition. I was a staff composer at McHale Barone, and Chris and Joe had done this commercial for Siemens Electronics in Europe, which caught the attention of the Jorgen Hausler who was creative director at the time. So he invited them to the pitch. They invited me to the pitch. Jorgen came over, showed me the brand guidelines, and he said, "We got a bunch of gray squares. We got these pink Ts. We don't know how many squares there are going to be. We don't know what order they're going to be in or anything like that." So I just developed a stupid simple algorithm of if you see a gray square, it's going to be a middle C. If you see a pink T, it'll be the E above it. So whatever order it came in, it would always work. So it could be "Ba da da da da," or "Ba da da da da," of "Ba da da da da da." That was it. That's the whole story.[5]

So it really only took 15 seconds? How does that happen?

My unfortunately late partner, Dr. Horowitz, he got me on to the concept of multimodal association, where it's like you associate the visuals with the audio, or a movement with a sound, or anything like that. And I just naturally was inclined that way. So the whole thing of, "Oh, I'll just associate the gray squares with the pink Ts." Right? And every time I've done anything remotely like this, I've always just fallen back on there's going to be emotion, there's going to be a color or something that can be associated with sound and movement. And just always start from there. And usually it's not that complicated a process. After that, it just becomes a matter of personal taste, do the creative directors like it?[6]

Why does he think we're still talking about it?

I don't know. I really don't know. I woke up one day a few years ago and realized I have been played more than any composer in history, right? Hundreds of millions of times a day that logo's going off somewhere. And I mean obviously the biggest part of it is the fact that T-Mobile are successful, and they keep throwing money at it. I mean, I wish they'd throw it at me, but that's a huge part of the success. I think the serendipity of the simplicity of their visual logo combined with the simplicity of the audio logo and how well they worked together, that probably plays a big part of it. But this is all conjecture on my part. I honestly don't have an answer for why it says successful. To me it was just another piano riff that I walked over and played.[7]

And what does he think of now when he hears it?

You would ask. I think, "There's me not getting paid again." That's what I think. Oh, geez. Yeah. It's tough one. My wife brings it up every few months. It's like, "Why aren't you getting royalties for that?" And I'm like, "That was the deal."[8]

Did he know then that we'd still be talking about it and it would still be being played?

Nobody could have known. I mean, T-Mobile at that time was a little company somewhere in Germany. Well, a big company, but only in Germany. It wasn't until after I've signed the contract that the next year after that they rolled out around the world and bought up all the cell phone carriers. So nobody knew. I mean, they probably knew how big they were going to get, but nobody outside of that did.[9]

Does he think that it's even more relevant today? Not only his sonic logo, but all sonic logos? Why don't more brands have them?

I don't understand why it's still an uphill battle. Why sonic branding is still an uphill battle. Why we have to educate people as to why it matters. Sound is so directly connected to emotions. And it's not subconscious, it's preconscious. The auditory system in the brain works so fast. It's like you hear a stick snap behind you. Before you can even think, you've turned around, your heart rate's up, your pupils are dilated, you are ready to go. Right? And that all happens in less than, I think, what is it, 20 milliseconds? Right? And to me for brands to not take advantage of that kind of power, I just don't get it. So I'm a huge proponent of sonic branding and because sound tweaks the emotion so much, it's like, a prime example, Virgin airlines. You get out of your Uber to go into the door and you head up to the counter. There should be some kind of soundscape there that makes you feel you're safe. You interact with the people at the counter. They should have some sort of soundscape around them. It doesn't have to be music can be music to make you feel safe and to make you feel like, "Oh, the Virgin experience is a fantastic experience." Right? Because at the end of the day, every brand touch point, all that matters is how you feel when you walk away. And will you remember it later? And by far the most effective way to do that is with sound. So it boggles my mind why we still have to educate people about this.[10]

What are some of his favorite sonic logos?

I have to confess, I only watch movies now. I have not seen a commercial in years. But let me, let me kind of rack the brain. I mean, obviously Walter's

[Werzowa] logo [Intel]. Because Walter's logo ticks all the boxes that I do, which is, it's got that motion, it interacts directly with the visuals. The four syllables, the four notes, the way you pronounce the words, all of that. By far, the classic NBC logo is still the godfather of us all. Recently, and actually a funny story, one logo which ticks all my boxes, I mean they did everything that I thought, and to me it was a major fail, was Honda. Because they've got the piano notes "Ba-da," like, "Aah," it hurt. But I can't tell you why. I mean all the things that go through my head whenever I'm trying to create something, they did exactly what I would've done, but they came up with something that I would not have presented to a client. And let's see. I haven't seen anything recently that really makes me think, "Wow, these guys nailed it." Or "That's going to live forever."[11]

Any others?

Actually, yeah. Netflix. That's a good one. Because it's got the weight behind it. There's just such a power in those sounds. I consider it more of a sound design. I forgot about Dr. Moorer [THX]. I used to be a big fan of his way back in the early days. I forget the name of that machine he invented for Lucas [Audio Signal Processor]. I remember back in the 1980s when I was still heavily into the academic side of things, I was reading *Computer Music Journal* back when it was a technical paper, and god, I cannot remember the name of that machine that he developed for them [ASP]. But it was amazing. It was a beautiful piece of work. Yeah. I got down into the circuit diagrams, into the math and all of that, and just was pulling the whole thing apart and wished that I had the budget to get one.[12]

You were at NeuroPop when you did the T-Mobile logo right?

NeuroPop started officially right after this logo, but I've been friends with Dr. Horowitz, jeez since I was 22 or 23, so at the time it had already been 20 years that we've known each other. And then this logo, like I said, he introduced me to the idea of multimodal association. And then so I asked him, I said, "Hey, can we do this with other things? Can we actually create sounds to mess with people's heads?" And being an auditory neuroscientist and a little bit crazy, he said, "Sure." And so that started that adventure. And actually our biggest success with that got rolled into an app called Sleepy Genius where we developed algorithms and techniques for naturally inducing sleep. And that did quite well. And it actually reached number one in the app store for a moment. We released some art projects, and I'm still carrying on some that... He passed away back in January, but I'm still carrying on some of his work. We developed audio algorithms for pain relief, and so I'm trying to figure out how to commercialize that.[13]

Why has he and others moved into music and health?

I mean I can't speak for the others, but if I was going to say there's a common thread, it's that as creatives, but as analytical people, the medical profession is an easy transition because there is all the tech behind medicine. And I can't say it about all musicians, but of the people you've mentioned, there's a caring that goes on. So it seems like a natural transition. It's like we care about how people feel. We care about using our skills to improve lives. We love the technology. In my case, I love programming and computers and I would say in Walter's case he came from a family of doctors, so he was probably just genetically inclined to be a healthcare provider. I mean obviously I'm speaking out of turn, speaking for Walter, but that's my inclination.[14]

Does he think that music has color or there's a color to represent a notes?

To me it's more about, again, it is the association, but it's the shape of things, right? So the gray square and the pink T to go back to T-Mobile. And Jorgen actually emphasized this. He said, "There is a specific ratio between the height of the square and the height of the T." And so I translated that dimension and sound. So for me it's not so much color as it is the space of things or the shape of things, or how they move through space and time. So for me personally, it would be much easier to create the sound of a triangle than it would be to create the sound of red.[15]

Finally, any funny stories? Does he use the logo to get him into fine restaurants?

So far, not for restaurant reservations, nobody knows me. I have used it to open doors. I've got a commercial representative right now who's

Courtesy of Maxim Media Inc.

shopping some of my songs for TV shows, and a big selling point is that he's the guy that wrote T-Mobile. And so people pay attention. Right? But in terms of is it stuck in my ear, my favorite one of those was *Maxim* magazine. Their 100th issue. They did a spot on me and it opened up with meet Lance Massey, the sadistic bastard that unleashed the T-Mobile audio logo. It was only like one column, but it was funny. But I just thought it was funny the way they started it out. And so that's how I'm known.[16]

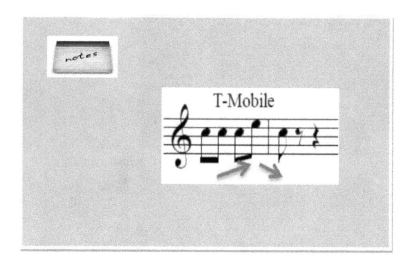

CHAPTER 8

McDonald's (2003)

Used with permission from the McDonald's Corporation.

It may not have saved McDonald's, but it sure helped it get is rhythm back ... and they have been Lovin' It ever since.

Eager to capitalize on a crumb of sales momentum after years of shortfalls, foul-ups and blunders, the McDonald's Corporation is taking a new creative direction in its advertising and marketing, based on persuading fast-food fans to rekindle their onetime love affair with the struggling restaurateur. The ambitious effort by McDonald's, described yesterday in a conference call with reporters, is encapsulated by a theme that will be introduced worldwide in the fall: "I'm lovin' it." The campaign will be the first in which the company commits itself to a comprehensive consolidated effort with a single idea shared globally, yet interpreted to suit local

markets at the same time. The new theme of the campaign, sched-
uled to run at least two years, will replace the many slogans now
seen and heard in 118 countries, including "Smile," the exhorta-
tion aimed at Americans since last year. McDonald's spends about
$1.5 billion a year in advertising, about half of that in the United
States. "The hope that consumers will soon resume singing "Can't
help lovin'" that McDonald's of mine," as Oscar Hammerstein II
might have phrased it, is a result of an unprecedented four-month
beauty pageant among 14 agencies that work for McDonald's in
10 major countries. They were asked to present creative concepts
that could travel beyond their borders. The "I'm lovin' it" idea was
the brainchild of a German agency, Heye & Partner, part of the
DDB Worldwide division of the Omnicom Group. Heye, based
in Munich, has created campaigns for McDonald's in Austria and
Germany since 1971. Jürgen Knauss, chief executive at Heye, said:
"The challenge was a tough one," Mr. Knauss said. "A key insight
was that a visit to McDonald's is one of the simplest pleasures of
everyday life." As for his agency's idea winning the McDonald's
beauty pageant, as it were, Mr. Knauss said, "I wouldn't be honest
if I didn't say it was a great moment."[1]

McDonald's Corp.'s choice of a little-known German agency called
Heye & Partner to lead its new worldwide ad campaign raised more
than a few industry eyebrows. After all, Heye is only the fifteenth largest
agency in Germany, an ad market that has long suffered a reputation for
lacking creativity. One can still spark a lively debate among German ad
executives by asking them whether humor is a useful tool in advertising.
But led by Chief Executive Jurgen Knauss, an energetic 65-year-old pipe
aficionado, Heye has doggedly worked to win the trust of McDonald's.
In Germany, Heye is so associated with the burger chain that people
sometimes call it "the McDonald's agency." Even before the recent triumph, the ads created by Heye for Germany have proved to be some of
McDonald's most exportable. In one lighthearted spot, a man is stuck
in a traffic jam and a kid in another car keeps making faces at him. For
revenge, the man holds up his pack of McDonald's fries and makes a show

of eating them. The spot or variations of it ran in 34 other markets from Europe to Hong Kong (though not in the United States). "They have a track record for coming up with great ideas that can travel," says Dean Barrett, global brand business officer for McDonald's. That relationship paid off when Heye came up with the winning tagline, "I'm lovin' it," in a worldwide idea bake-off McDonald's held among 14 agencies this year. McDonald's will let each country decide whether to use "I'm lovin' it" in English or the vernacular. When Chairman and CEO Jim Cantalupo took the reins of the world's largest restaurant company, he blamed, in part, poor marketing for the doldrums, despite the fact that McDonald's is one of the world's biggest advertisers, spending hundreds of millions of dollars a year on the brand. A month later Mr. Cantalupo summoned its largest ad agencies, including those from Omnicom's DDB Worldwide and Publicis Groupe SA's Leo Burnett, to its headquarters in Oak Brook, IL, for a creative shoot-out. Heye, which is part of the DDB network, triumphed in June, when McDonald's announced its winning tagline. "It's more than a line," says Charlie Bell, McDonald's chief operating officer. "It's a brand attitude"[2]

> Ever since McDonald's introduced "I'm lovin" it' as its first global advertising theme last September, some people have wondered whether the message would fail, suggesting that anything from cold fries to sluggish service could undermine its authority. But yesterday, eight months into the "I'm lovin' it" regime, McDonald's executives described a new round of 13 commercials from agencies around the world in which the theme remains nothing but love. They described, too, a world in which the jingle that accompanies "I'm lovin' it" springs forth from cellphones, wind chimes and sports arenas. "The phrase 'I'm lovin' it' is becoming part of the language," said Larry Light, executive vice president and global chief marketing officer at McDonald's, based in Oak Brook, Ill. "The campaign, the attitude and all of our integrated marketing have helped dramatically." Beyond traditional advertising, McDonald's also hopes to build the five-note tune that accompanies "I'm lovin' it" on television and radio into an "audio logo," as Mr. Light put it.[3]

Bill Lamar was the Chief Marketing Officer at McDonald's from 2002 to 2008 and began there in 1984. He worked at McDonald's from March, 1984 to March, 2008. He currently in the President of WBAL, LLC a marketing consulting firm in Atlanta, Georgia. He has an MBA in Marketing from the Kellogg School of Management at Northwestern University and a Bachelor's Degree in Political Science from the University of Illinois at Chicago. He currently resides in Atlanta, Georgia.

What was McDonald's thinking back then?

Well, if you go back to that time period, we really had poor business results for several years. We made a change in management and began developing what came to be called in McDonald's "The Plan to Win," which basically focused in on how we were going to change our strategy, to be able to regain our leadership in the quick service restaurant business. I won't spend a lot of time on "the plan to win," but one major component of it was to truly focus on our customers' needs and wants. We had a tendency in McDonald's to focus internally, focus on what it was that we wanted to achieve, as opposed to what it was that the customer needed or wanted from us. Part and parcel of that in marketing was developing, a customer-centric, customer-focused marketing and communications plan. The CMO of the global organization was a gentleman named Larry Light. Understand McDonald's structure. There was a global organization that oversaw four different geographic divisions around the world. And the division that I was responsible for in marketing, the United States, was the largest division. Larry and I worked well together and we both came to the point of view that obviously we needed to modernize and become more contemporary in our communications and organizations. As a result of that, Larry instituted a worldwide competition among all of our agencies. McDonald's had over 80 agencies worldwide at the time many of whom were affiliated with two holding companies, Omnicom and Publicus. One of the Omnicon agencies, ultimately won. And that was Heye & Partners in Unterhaching Germany. Two young guys came up came up with the slogan, "I'm lovin' it" and also decided to make the musical foundation of it hip hop. A pretty radical idea for a "family values" brand like McDonald's in 2002. We narrowed down the ideas. At one point in the process there were over 40 ideas. We narrowed them down to 10. And "I'm lovin' it" really resonated with us. And it resonated with us because it was simple. It was customer-focused; it was speaking from the customer's perspective on McDonald's. And the architecture of it was very modern. Also, the ability to use not only hip hop, but any musical genre around that slogan, was very appealing to us. So we chose it. And the agency, I think was a 10-person agency at the time, was shocked, as you might imagine. But it just goes to show you, ideas come from people and individuals, they don't come from organizations and bureaucracies. And that was the origin of "I'm lovin' it." One of the important things we did, and this is really, I think, the area that you're focusing on, was really work on what was going to make it memorable? And so there are two things that we look at in marketing on memorability, and both of them are mnemonics. You call one of them audio. I think of them as mnemonics. For McDonald's the colors red and yellow are iconic to the McDonald's brand; actually it's yellow and red. And then we wanted to find an audio, oral, mnemonics as well. And that's how dadadadada was developed. The science behind that you probably know better than I do. But the fact of the matter is, that sound, that mnemonic is very important. If you think about advertising and you think about the environments that advertising is in, often people aren't listening or paying attention, even though the ad is running or visible. Whether it's on their phone, on their television, on their watch, people's attentions are often in other places. And so the more you can have something that signifies your brand and grabs their attention the more likelihood you have of being able to communicate whatever message is that you're trying to communicate. And so that was the rationale for having as much focus as we did on a mnemonic like dadadadada.[4]

How did Justin Timberlake and Pharrell Williams become part of the strategy?

Well, we made music central to the idea and central to the campaign. And I will tell you that the selection of Justin Timberlake to be the talent for the initial rollout of the campaign was quite interesting. At that point in time, he was an up-and-comer. He hadn't yet achieved the fame, he has today. I questioned using him, given that the music foundation fundamentally was hip-hop, and he was not a hip-hop artist. He was not even in the hip-hop genre. A gentleman named Steve Stoute recommended him. I sat and talked with Steve. He persuaded me Justin would work and we went forward. It turned out to be great. The music was central to every idea. I don't even think we did a commercial in the first year or two that didn't have a music bed. I could be wrong, but I doubt it. Music allowed us to be contemporary and also allowed us to be demographically targeted based on who we're trying to reach. Up until that point, the average customer viewed the McDonald's brand as trusted and friendly but actually, kind of old stodgy. We'd been around a long time and we weren't viewed as being young or vibrant or contemporary; on the edge of what younger customers would find appealing. So music was very important in helping to change that perception. Also the visuals, the editing that we used with our commercials was also very important. It was quick, it was multiple visuals, multiple scenes, energetic music, but energetic music in every genre. The great thing about "I'm lovin' it," the music itself, is that it can be adopted to Country and Western. It can be adopted to Pop. It could be adopted today, to K-pop if you wanted it to.[5]

This was when Timberlake was going solo right?

Well, it was actually part of his marketing, if you will, because he was an up-and-comer and his label and his folks were pushing him to be a star. And so doing a McDonald's commercial that was going to get as much exposure as this one was, was a win for him and a win for us. The campaign cost was over a billion dollars in the United States. I'll tell you an interesting story. When I sat down and I talked with Steve Stoute about Timberlake. I was not a fan of Justin Timberlake being of our vocal talent. This was a hip-hop-based idea and Timberlake had no credibility in hip-hop. And so, I didn't know Steve, at the time. I called a mutual friend and said, "tell me about this guy. I want to meet him." And so he and I sat down and had a drink. And the first thing out of my mouth was "How the hell can you recommend Justin Timberlake to be the talent introducing our new campaign?" And it went from there; half an hour later he had me convinced. So thank goodness I figured out how to listen. In McDonald's, the idea of having hip hop as the basis of a national campaign was not without controversy. McDonald's USA is a compilation of owner operators, employees, and restaurant managers around the country and it reflects the different parts of the country. And in Wyoming or Alabama the folks weren't as enthusiastic about hip-hop in those days, as the folks in New York or L.A.. Now the reality is, their children were loving it. And that's where we were targeting and focusing; young adults. But we had more than a few conversations with Owners of McDonald's around the country who had trepidation about our association with hip hop. Over the years, really in particularly the first two or three years, quite a number of different talents were used within the campaign. Actually, Justin was really the face of it for several months. And then his agreement was over and we moved on. but he helped us accomplish what we needed to accomplish, which was to get attention, start changing how people viewed the McDonald's brand. And for us, the most important thing to make us younger. We did a lot of work around the brand positioning or brand essence of being "forever young." The McDonald's brand should be "forever young." And we had that permeate, not just what we did marketing wise, but also brand wide, the change in restaurant architecture and building design, was based on that. So everything we did, we wanted it to feel young, contemporary, with the times, and that all came out of "I'm lovin it."[6]

It seems like McDonald's shares a similar sonic strategy as does another Atlanta corporation: Coca-Cola right?

Oh yeah, we are their largest customer. We have a great relationship. I'll tell you a quick story. Up until about 10 years ago... McDonald's and Coca-Cola go back to 1955. Up until about 10 years ago, there was never a written contract with Coca-Cola and McDonald's, it was all on a handshake.[7]

Why are we all still so interested in this sonic logo?

Well, I think it's several things. Number one, it's simple and easy to remember, and it relates, it relates to the brand that it represents. Number two, we'd been relentless, I can't speak as much lately, but we were relentless in communicating the "I'm lovin' it" message. We spent billions of dollars, communicating that message. And we did it in compelling ways.

We had some bombs, but by and large, we executed it pretty well. The third is it relates to the brand. It relates to how people use McDonald's. Now it's not an intense, "I'm lovin' it." It's a fun, joyful kind that fits your every day "I'm lovin' it." Easy to say, good mnemonics around it, good execution of having it come to life, tactically.[8]

What does he think of when he hears it now?

Oh my goodness. It was so ubiquitous with me that I don't even... to be honest, I don't think much of anything. I've heard it so often, and know so much about it. I admire the folks who have continued to keep it modern, keep it fresh, keep it contemporary so that it still resonates with folks. And I think that's the longevity of it, is that it's a positioning and it's a slogan that can be timeless, as long as the execution of it and the communication of it is current. And so, I look at it that way. And quite honestly, I still find myself surprised from time to time that it's still there. Usually when new marketing people come in, they want to do their own thing. And, it says something to the strength of what the guys from Unterhaching Germany came up with that it's still around.[9]

Anything that he would like to share with future CMOs?

I would just say a couple of things to them and wish them the best. First, it is about whoever your customer is. And if you're the marketer, you are the customer's advocate, you are the customer's voice, not your voice, based on what you have learned about your customer. You've got to be that voice in your organization for your organization to have sustained success. That'd be the first thing. Second, I would say to them is, as a marketer, know your entire business model, not just what the communications and marketing aspects. Understand how your business makes a profit. Be knowledgeable about financial aspect of the business model. Understand how you recruit and retain great talent, Understand management principles. It'll make you as a marketer, much stronger. It will add to your credibility and give you more leverage to achieve and get done, within your company. Don't allow yourself to be pigeonholed as just the marketing guy or gal. People do that. And in most companies, that's a pigeon hole that means they only come to you when they need sales or things are bad. Why can't we get more customers in there? Fix our brands' image. We need to do this. And you're a miracle worker, and there aren't very many miracles. So I would just say, make sure that you're grounded in the totality of your business and that your peers and superiors recognize that. And it'll make your marketing much stronger, because you'll understand, much better what it is that you have, that a customer wants or conversely what you don't have that the customer needs.[10]

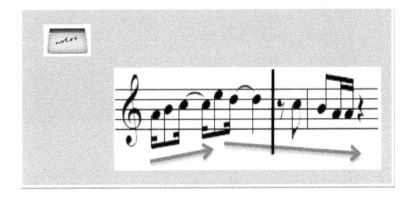

CHAPTER 9

Coca-Cola (2006 and 2016)

Courtesy of Coca-Cola.

From McDonald's we move to Coca-Cola with one more great sonic strategy and two more sonic logos from two creators Umut Ozaydinli and Joe Belliotti.

The notes for "Open Happiness" first appeared in "Happiness Factory," a 2006 TV commercial and online film imagining the whimsical, animated world inside a Coca-Cola vending machine. The award-winning spot, which spawned several sequels in the years that followed, came to life through brilliant animation and a cinematic soundscape. "In 2007, as we were developing the 'Open Happiness' campaign, we wanted an audio branding device similar to the ones used by McDonald's and Intel," explains Nick Felder, Coke's global director of film and music production. "We went through our existing library of music assets, and it quickly became obvious that the hook we were looking for could be found in the spine of the melody of the 'Happiness Factory' score, which was running in every market." The team distilled the 15-note melody from the film to a five-note mnemonic, then tested it with different instruments and in different keys and tempos. One of the first Coke TV spots to feature the new signature was "Share the Love." The five notes can be heard punched on a telephone keypad at the end of the 2007 ad. The "Open Happiness" single, which featured Cee-Lo Green, Patrick Stump of Fall Out Boy, Brendon Urie of Panic at the Disco, Travis McCoy of Gym Class Heroes, and Grammy-nominated songstress Janelle Monae was the first original song to include the melody. The uplifting collaboration was released in 2009, and 24 versions were recorded in different languages and released in more than 30 countries. Since then, the five notes have been featured in literally hundreds of Coca-Cola anthems, including Mark Ronson and Katy B's "Anywhere in the World," which anchored the "Move to the Beat campaign" for the London 2012 Olympic Games, One Night Only's "Can You Feel it Tonight" from 2011, and holiday-themed tracks from 2010 (Train's "Shake Up Christmas"), 2011 (Natasha Bedingfield's mutilingual take on the same tune), and 2012 ("Something in the Air", performed by Grayson Sanders, Lauriana Mae and Jono). The melody provides a full bar of recognizable music that fits easily into most pop time signatures, opening the door to genre-spanning adaptations around the world. The most successful use of the melody, to date, was K'Naan's "Wavin Flag." Coke's anthem for the 2010 FIFA World Cup in South Africa topped the charts in 17 countries and created a festive call to action for football fans to chant and sing during matches. "When the song would play in stadiums, crowds would spontaneously shout the chorus in the form of a cheer," Felder says. "The first time we realized the song would go viral was when we saw a cell phone video on YouTube of the Brazilian football team psyching themselves up before a match by singing the five-note melody on a stadium concourse in Rio."[1]

Several years ago, Coca-Cola made a significant shift in their marketing strategy, announcing that, for the first time ever, all four colas would be marketed under one brand. Building on this success, we rolled out this strategy globally and launched a new creative campaign and tagline, "Taste the Feeling." Chief Marketing Officer Marcos de Quinto,

TASTE THE FEELING®

Courtesy of Coca-Cola.

who unveiled the "one brand" approach, said the strategy extends the equity and iconic appeal of the world's No. 1 beverage brand to Coca-Cola Light / Diet Coca-Cola, Coca-Cola Zero, and Coca-Cola Life. The new approach also underscores our commitment to choice, offering consumers whichever Coca-Cola suits their taste, lifestyle and diet—with or without calories, with or without caffeine. "We are reinforcing that Coca-Cola is for everybody," de Quinto said. "Coca-Cola is one brand with different variants, all of which share the same values and visual iconography. People want their Coca-Cola in different ways, but whichever one they want, they want a Coca-Cola brand with great taste and refreshment." "Taste the Feeling" brings to life the idea that drinking a Coca-Cola—any Coca-Cola—is a simple pleasure that makes everyday moments more special. While our award-winning "Open Happiness" campaign leaned heavily on what the brand stands for over the last seven years, "Taste the Feeling" employs universal storytelling with the product at the heart to reflect both the functional and emotional aspects of the Coca-Cola experience. "We've found over time that the more we position Coca-Cola as an icon, the smaller we become," de Quinto said. "The bigness of Coca-Cola resides in the fact that it's a simple pleasure – so the humbler we are, the bigger we are. We want to help remind people why they love the product as much as they love the brand." The fully integrated "Taste the Feeling" campaign uses authentic storytelling to celebrate the experience of drinking an ice-cold Coca-Cola. Coca-Cola takes center stage in every piece of what Rodolfo Echeverria, VP of global creative, connections and digital, calls "emotional product communication." "We've gone from 'Open Happiness' to exploring the role Coca-Cola plays in happiness," he added. "We make simple, everyday moments more special." An international network of agencies developed the "Taste the Feeling" work. Four agencies—Mercado-McCann, Santo, Sra. Rushmore and Ogilvy & Mather—produced an initial round of 10 TV commercials, digital, print, out-of-home, and shopper materials. The "Taste the Feeling" TV ads offer intimate glimpses into universal stories, feelings, and everyday moments people share while enjoying Coca-Cola. At the close of each spot, the family of Coca-Cola products unite under the iconic red Coca-Cola disc. Several alternate versions of the ads were produced with locally relevant casts and culturally relevant vignettes. The campaign kicked off with the lead commercial, "Anthem," which presents a series of moments linked by a Coca-Cola, such as ice-skating with friends, a first date, a first kiss, and a first love. An original song performed by Conrad Sewell serves as the ad's soundtrack and "Taste the Feeling" campaign anthem, continuing Coke's legacy of using iconic music in its advertising. The track includes an audio signature inspired by the sounds of enjoying a Coca-Cola—the pop of the cap, the fizz and, ultimately, refreshment. The pneumonic replaces the five-note melody featured in the "Open Happiness" campaign. Avicii, a longtime Coca-Cola collaborator, played a key role in the development of the "Taste the Feeling" anthem.[2]

We talked with two former Global Heads of Music at Coca-Cola: Umut Ozaydinli and Joe Belliotti.

Umut is an expert in disruption, branding and entertainment marketing. He has spent the last 20 years combining music, film, technology, and popular culture to create extraordinary global campaigns for international brands and has won several awards for his work. Since the beginning of his career, the *Fast Company*-christened "wild Turk" has applied his unique branding skills to beverage giant Coca-Cola and myriad other brands, including Bacardi, Nestea, MTV, and Avon. As Coca-Cola's Global Head of Music and as head of Deviant Ventures, he orchestrated music marketing campaigns for global events, such as the FIFA World Cup, the Olympics and UEFA Eurocup. The single that he created for Coca-Cola's 2010 FIFA World Cup campaign made number one in over 19 countries reaching to 150 countries and delivering 100 million views on YouTube. The single he produced to launch Coca-Cola's new global campaign "Taste the Feeling" featuring Avicii, is one of the most popular videos on Coke's YouTube channel with over 22 million views with 50 million streams on Spotify.[3]

In 2019 Joe co-founded The Music Division, working with established and emerging brands to amplify and extend their strategies through music. Joe was most recently the Head of Global Music at The Coca-Cola Company, where he created global and scalable content, platforms, partnerships, capabilities and strategies for brands across the company's portfolio. Previously Joe established entertainment marketing firm Brand Asset Group as a leader in providing insight-led strategies, creative ideation and execution of integrated marketing partnerships developed through the lens of entertainment and pop culture for Fortune 500 and celebrity brands. Earlier in his career, Joe worked in talent development at the music publishing arm of Maverick (a Madonna/Warner Bros. joint venture). He has also been a music supervisor for film & TV projects for Warner Bros TV and ABC.[4]

Why did Coca-Cola switch from Open Happiness to Taste the Feeling, Umut?

So the issue with the five-note melody was you were not able to sing the tagline. It was very cute. It was very topical, but you can't. And so if our marketers, our challenge is to increase the awareness for the tagline for next 10 years to come out, at least that was the intention at the time. We should change the tagline in a way that we bring in the tagline in a more sing-able way. Then second, maybe this might be even bigger priority, was one of the objectives of that campaign, specifically, was remind people the intrinsic pleasure of consuming Coca-Cola, intrinsic versus the extrinsic. So that's where the tagline came from Taste the Feeling, remind people how amazing and how refreshing it is to drink Coca-Cola. Now we, obviously, we're super-lucky with Coca-Cola because it has a soundscape around the consumption. You open the cap, you hear the bubbles, you hear the ice, you pour it. So, we basically get a lot of inspiration and use from the soundscape that the product consumption had and bake that into our audio melody as organically as possible. I can send you examples of it. When you hear the audio melody, it's always the cap opening. You here, the fizz and, "Ahh," it's almost like, "Oh my God, I really need to have a drink, a Coca-Cola." I don't know if you would be familiar, but there is this awards in Europe called Red Dot awards. They are technically industrial design and design awards. And recent years they also introduced audio design as one of the fields, and audio logos is one of the fields. And we actually won a Red Dot award with our audio melody, which when you look into different types of awards, this is probably one of the most rigorous award in the industry because they are not looking into just like, "Oh this is like a very catchy tune." No, they are looking much more strategically, "Wow, this actually has so much strategy and thinking behind it." It's design thinking used to basically address a marketing challenge.[5]

Joe continued.

You can go back to 1920s when Coke first went on the radio is when you start seeing Coke use music and sound. And it's funny, the Taste the Feeling, the approach we took, which has the intrinsic sounds of Coke, the bubbles and the ice and the sounds of Coke, that was actually used back in the 1940s and 1950s as well because we were putting out the same messaging into the market. So back into the 1940s and 1950s, the messaging around Coke in the United States was, "Have an ice cold Coke. It's refreshing." So they wanted to talk about the product a lot. So they actually used a lot of sounds, especially because radio needs to advertise. So they used a lot of those sounds. Then you got into the 1960s, and in the sixties you there was a campaign called, "Things go better with Coke," which was the more of a tagline of a lyric tagline that was given to the music industry. And artists like James Brown, Aretha Franklin, The Who, massive artists created songs called "Things Go Better with Coke," and they use that line in all different ways in their music, so that was sort of a really interesting one. In the 1970s, of course there was like, "I'd like to buy the world a Coke," which had the song, "I'd like to teach the world to sing." So those two things lived together in the 1970s. In the 1980s you had Always Coca-Cola, which was very, very popular, very memorable jingle. So there's been a lot of uses of music. And I think when you get into Open Happiness, Open Happiness is one of those sort of, I think, just really defined that era of Coke like those other ones did, I'd like to think, because of the way it was adopted and used the pop culture. On this point, Taste the Feeling was very specific. We had gone back to that very product-centric marketing. We wanted to remind people about the product of Coke. And Coke, when you look at it, you recognize Coke when you see it. You recognize Coke when you hold the bottle. The actual brief to create the contour bottle over a hundred years ago was they wanted a shape that someone could touch in the dark and recognize. So you could recognize Coke when you see it, and you recognize Coke when you taste it. Coke has a very unique taste. The flavor profile of Coke is actually very unique. It's hard to replicate. And you recognize Coke when you hear it. So we wanted to go back to that, "Let's make sure people recognize Coke when they hear it." And when you hear Coke, to Umut's point earlier, we took the entire journey of if you listen to what is on that video, we took the entire journey from like opening the fridge, grabbing the bottle out of the fridge, taking the bottle. You hear ambient noises because you're hanging out with people, it's social. You get the bottle, you pop off the cap, you hear the cap fall, you hear the fizz. You hear the liquid pour over the ice, you hear it crackling. You hear that sort of white noise that the fizz makes. Then you hear the gulp of the drink, and then you hear the, "Ah." So it's the entire experience of drinking a Coke that we captured. And then we had to sort of put it into different time lengths to fit different uses. I'll try to find some videos, but it was definitely something that popped up quite a bit in the 1940s and 1950s.[6]

Umut continued.

To tell the story of Taste the Feeling, you really have to start from the Open Happiness because it's a journey over, perhaps, a span of 15 years or so. What Joe explained in terms of the story is actually the precursor of Open Happiness. At the time when we launched Open Happiness, which was a very different campaign than the previous campaign, which was received magnificently well, and that was exactly when I joined the global team at Coca Cola. We had this update meeting with the CEO of the Coca Cola at the time to tell how great we are doing as marketers on this campaign. We had all the TV spots, and this is basically the campaign which introduced the Happiness Factory, the iconic Happiness Factory. And there was so many amazing commercials in the portfolio with that campaign, including a TV spot with Jack White, et cetera. So it was very interesting. The CEO listened to the presentation and said like, "Guys, apologies, you guys as marketers are telling me this is the best campaign of all times. But if you look at historically all of the Coca Cola campaigns, you can hum the campaign. I can't hum this campaign. There is no melody associated with it." And it was then that we basically get the charge from the CEO, and we looked back and said, "Oh, you know what? He's right. All of the iconic Coca-Cola campaigns over the existence is associated with a melody that you can't forget, like "Always Coca-Cola," it's part of my childhood." It's impossible. I might forget all the TV spots that I had seen around Always Coca-Cola, but I will not forget that melody. I won't remember one TV spot with that campaign, but I will remember that melody. And as marketers, at that point we realized, "Oh, yeah, we have to have a melody. That's basically what will make the campaign more memorable and remember it." And as marketeers, when you're working at a brand iconic as Coca-Cola is, spending billions of dollars of marketing, so it's not what you're doing today, but will it be remembered in the history of the brand as well? So we started the journey. Here's the thing, TV spots, technically speaking, are an annoyance. People do not connect with the TV spot, but music is something, or melodies is something that's so ingrained in our hearts in our mind. It's something that allows us to connect with either the message or the brand. So I think that goes all under the same umbrella. It basically is a very effective way to create affinity and get people to connect with the campaign. So once we get the mandate from the CEO, we started the search, like every other company would do, "Okay let's bring some music houses. Let's basically start bringing some demos in and stuff like that." But also one thing we realized at the time, one of our TV spots was charting, getting scores off the charts, which was Happiness Factory. And at the time at least, and I'm sure they change it a million times, when you look at the score of a TV spot you'll basically break it down to different elements. What it's like, why it's like. And one of the things on that TV spot, on the first Happiness Factory TV spot was the melody. People just loved the melody. It was obviously very lovable characters on the screen as well, but people really loved the melody. So we basically, after doing a long journey with the film and production department of Coca-Cola at the time, we come to the conclusion, the best melody we had in our hand was the melody that we already started using with the Happiness Factory because it's also one of these things when you're introducing a melody like this one, especially in an international scale, it's not always easy to get buy-in from international markets. And now we have this TV spot that everyone is wanting and it was scoring everywhere so well we said, "Okay, it just makes sense. Let's basically convert the five notes melody that is in use in this TV spot to our audio signature." Now because it was more of a tactical move, perhaps a reaction, no one really talked about, "Oh, can you sing the Coca-Cola brand melody? Or can you add a message or tagline, something like that with it?" It was much more reactionary versus strategic, but it worked out because it was such a catchy tune. And we basically managed to develop and build it throughout the years in a very effective way. Well, once again, I'm going back to the same story. One of the things at the time, basically when the time came for us to launch the melody, we basically wanted to make it famous. We were working with the second installation of Happiness Factory when we were ready to launch. How can you make a melody famous? We said,

> Okay, what if we bring few artists that already is in pop culture that our audience love. We create a song that is almost extension of the campaign, but it is an actual song, almost like a single. If we use this as a launch platform to launch the melody, it probably will be better than just launching with the TV spot.

So in conjunction with that, we did a single that featured Ceelo Green, Janell Monae, Fallout Boy, Panic at the Disco, Travis McCoy from Gym Class Heroes, and actually that is the origin story of Joe Belliotti and Umut got started this is the first project we actually collaborated. And we always make this mind trick with people, Joe was the agency at that time, and I was the client. I was basically head of music partnerships at the time at Coca-Cola, and we basically did this, and it was supersuccessful. We were in charts all around the world with this melody. So it's progression of the same, basically, success. So, basically, we launched this, it was very good. Then the following year we had World Cup, and everyone turned to us and asked us, "Okay, World Cup is coming. It's our biggest campaign yet to come. You guys did a great job with launching the new audio logo in form of a single. Can you guys do something for the World Cup campaign that basically will bring it even further?" And we basically couldn't stop thinking, "Oh my God, like this is actually a very good chance because you can, it's very tractable." So we then followed and did another song for the next campaign coming in for the World Cup, which was still part of the same campaign, so you don't need to change the audio logo. And we did another song that basically it called for celebration, which, basically, our hope was will be chanted at the stadiums, which, it's rare case in marketing you start with a vision and you actually realize it. It happened. So next probably eight years or so was basically, "Oh, my god, this is basically a great way for us to launch campaigns and make people happy."[7]

Joe continued.

Well, I will say, before you skip eight years ahead, I think it's worth mentioning on Waving Flag, the reality is that was one of 40 things that were created for that campaign for marketing assets. 40 is not the accurate number, but probably 40 from digital assets to mobile to visuals to experiences, tons of content. It's the biggest campaign Coke had ever done, so there was a lot of marketing assets, and the music got no more attention than anything else. It was one of 40. And the reason it became one of the most used by Coca-Cola during the time, and the reason it became a number one song around the world, was because people gravitated it toward the music. We didn't put any media around the song itself except it was in a few commercials. It wasn't like we pushed the song into the market. It was really people gravitated toward it, which was amazing because they liked the song. But it was also, from a marketing perspective, it was an amazing value because we got so much out of it for relatively small investment when you think about traditional marketing.[8]

So thinking back, what does Joe remember most about the creation of Taste the Feeling?

So creating the Taste the Feeling audio logo, we actually had one talent that did everything, that played every instrument, was every sound. And it was great working with this talent because it always showed up on time, and it was the Coke bottle. We really took every single sound in that audio signature, was generated from the Coke bottle. And we didn't use it as an instrument. It's not like we were banging on it and trying to recreate drums. We were really just trying to take the sounds that the bottle and drinking a Coca-Cola make, from grabbing it to the fridge, to pouring it over the ice, to the fizz, to the refreshment. So everything was generated by the bottle. So, basically, it was an exercise of recording the bottle, doing what it does.[9]

Of all the logos it's probably the only sonic logo that the product itself actually created. Does Umut think that why it was so powerful?

I wouldn't say it is the only one because Coke had a big heritage of using intrinsic sounds in radio spots in different times and period. But what I would say, Taste the Feeling is probably one that we put much more strategy and intention on every aspect of it, from the melody allowing us to be able to sing the tagline, to basically bringing the strategic priority of the campaign, which was reminding people intrinsic pleasure and taste of drinking Coca-Cola using audio and all types of elements to bring it to life. Probably Coca-Cola, when you look in their existence, they use different elements, different times of the different campaigns. But probably we used it with much more intention and strategy because we had a very specific brief, remind people the simple pleasure of drinking Coca-Cola. And what is better to remind? Use an audio soundscape that everyone already familiar from their childhood, from their youth, opening the bottle, hearing the fizz, listening it pouring into the glass at the first sip, which is always the best sip.[10]

Joe agreed.

I think that's key, Umut, is that the sounds we use were actually very, very familiar. We all recognize them, just like we recognize the logo, we recognize the bottle shape. We recognize the sounds, and I think what we did is just put them together in a musical format.[11]

That is Coca-Cola's DNA, right Umut? Coca-Cola traditionally likes to create new sounds as opposed to getting a favorite artist at the time, or the sort of replicating something that they had done before, right?

I don't really think you can pick one pattern in the existence of a brand that is 130-plus years old because I think each different period that existed in history, they approach it very differently. Coca-Cola actually is one of the brands, probably the brand introduced what is called music endorsements to its first form and shape with engaging a bar hall singer. Joe will tell you the story a little bit better than I can do. Joe, do you want to tell them? When you look at Coca-Cola, a brand like Coca-Cola, they everything. Well, one point in time they did printed music and stuff like that. So I don't think we can say we are the first to basically use either the sound elements or some sort of catchy tune in a combination. But what I can say is, both Joe and I love history a lot. And when you are basically working with an iconic brand like Coca-Cola, one of the first things they do is they send you to the basement, which is one of the biggest corporate archives in the world. And you see how, basically, the same story has been told over years. So what I think we did is we had the luxury to pick and choose what we loved the best, what we felt people connected the most. And we brought it all together as organically as we can. It was not just the tagline sing-able, the soundscape used. We also engage up-and-coming talent to basically sing the parts. Now our bet was that gentlemen would be the next Bruno Mars, which in Australia he absolutely is, but he didn't break internationally as big as we want him to be. But we basically used so many different elements and tactics, it was a fun project for us to collaborate. And I think probably with between me and Joe, it marked our 10 years of collaborations when we did the Taste the Feeling. So it was almost like we were a very well-rehearsed team that basically know both sides of the story. And we, basically, had a great time digesting all of the learnings that Coca-Cola had over 130-plus years, and basically bringing what makes sense in today's world.[12]

Does Belliotti think sonic logos are even more important today with smart speakers and limited attention spans?

Well, I like to say, if people recognize your brand when they see it, are they going to recognize it when they hear it? Because people, the audiences are spending over 40 hours a week listening, whether it's music or podcasts or audio books or voice devices. When we start shopping on voice devices, that changes the entire dynamic of how people connect with the brand. You're getting into a year 2020 where half of all searches on Google will be voice searches. So what that means is that all the beautiful iconography, the packaging, the logos that were done, they don't translate into an audio environment. So I think audio sonic identities, more comprehensive approaches to sonic identities are a must for brands today.[13]

Umut agreed.

I couldn't agree more. Look, audio is going to emerge as the next interface in next five years, 10 years. We already have all my lights in the house is basically voice comment. When I want to hear the news, I'm asking to hear the news. So what's going to happen is our screen time will start going down because audio is much more intuitive. I'm not needing to look into my phone to give a command or read the news. I'm asking my Google assistant or Alexa to tell me. Then there's going to be commercials in between those. But it is one thing showing like a new car on a banner ad or a TV like a pre roll. It's another thing reminding a brand using audio to people and what that brand represents to you. Like BMW, for example, has certain brand elements that you would never hear it on audio or see it on the audio unless some intelligent marketer thought about it and say, "You know what? We are modern. We are this year that. We need to bring audio clues together in a way that when someone hears this audio or sound or whatever, that is what the emotion is awoke about my brand." And I think the next stage off audio branding is similar to what we have done. It's not just a catchy tune. There are so many bad catchy tunes like glorified jingles out there. But does that make you feel something about the brand? Yep. If you say Liberty, Liberty, Liberty Mutual, 10 times people will remember that was your ad. Great, you check one of the boxes. But I would argue, as marketers, our job is to build relationships,

emotional relationship with our audiences. And I think what the marketer will need to do more and more is find effective ways to articulate
what the brand stands for more efficiently than audio, is one aspect of
it, audio logos and audio melodies. We started introducing audio style
guidelines five, six years ago together with Joe in our time at Coca-Cola,
which was like people didn't initially understand why would we need a
style guide for melody? Well, because there are increasing different ways
your brand will need to interact with the audience. And the way you have
a design style guideline to tell you what not to do next to each color or
how to draw that box or logo, you need that for audio as well because
you're talking about the high end of the smart speakers. But your brand
will still need to exist in gazillion different way places, either TV spots,
radio spots, in-store if you have a smart device, and which we are going
to see more and more a switch that might have an audio cue adapt to it.
That was a long way to say it, but I agree with Joe.[14]

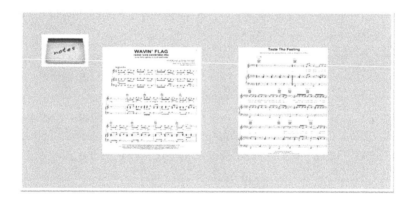

CHAPTER 10

AT&T (2012)

Courtesy of at&t.

We end on another good *note* and it's composer, Joel Beckerman. Joel Beckerman is an award-winning composer and producer for television. He is the founder of Man Made Music, a company specializing in sonic branding. *Fast Company* named him one of their "Most Creative People in Business" and Man Made Music one of their "Most Innovative Companies" in music. He created original scores for more than 50 television programs, won ASCAP's "Most Performed" theme award for the past eight years, and has developed signature sonic branding programs for global giants such as Disney, AT&T, and Southwest Airlines. Beckerman has worked with John Legend, will.i.am, Moby, OK Go, Morgan Freeman, and the composer John Williams. He lives in New Providence, New Jersey.[1]

One of his most ambitious projects was an 18-month stint creating a sonic logo and other musical signatures, including a soaring minute-and-a half anthem, for telecommunications giant AT&T. "Likening AT&T's new aural hook to its voice," Vice President of Brand Identity and Design Gregg Heard said, "We want you to hear us and know us even when you can't see us." AT&T declined to discuss the project's costs, but sonic-branding budgets typically

range between $60,000 and several hundred thousand dollars, professionals said. Beckerman said one of his biggest hurdles was distilling a single piece of music that would speak for all the company's varied operations, from consumer phone services to network infrastructure. He needed to convey friendliness to AT&T customers while also sounding a rally cry for its 256,000 employees. Unlike a singer-songwriter who might pour his heart into a composition, Beckerman's process is more empirical. "You have to understand the science before you do the art," he said. He started the AT&T project by surveying the competition, gathering more than 200 sonic logos, including Nextel's communications chirp. He discovered that virtually all of them used electronic tones and realized AT&T had the opportunity for a more earthy sounding alternative. He presented the company with relevant trends in art, music and culture. With a mandate to humanize AT&T, he spotlighted the way some consumers try to balance their tech-saturated lives with pursuits like organic foods, crafts and the often ramshackle sound of Brooklyn indie rock bands. He played music for his clients, including a song by the idiosyncratic British singer Imogen Heap, and had them rate it based on the mood conveyed. That gave him a better sense of what his client's parameters for "human"-sounding music were. During parts of the AT&T project, up to eight musicians wrote in groups in three small studios in the Man Made office. These teams tackled the task from different angles, Beckerman said, but all their work was measured against a one-page mission statement boiled down from the preparatory workshops with AT&T. Through three rounds of composition, they created 60 different pieces of music. Beckerman chose seven of them to present to AT&T. Though it was partly a gut decision, he said he tried to pick compositions that objectively conveyed a blend of attitudes, including "curious, open, inventive, purposeful," in keeping with the company's goals. One of the first songs built on slicing and sweeping notes from a string quartet. Its mood was grand but a little scary. Another sounded more homespun, with hand claps, chugging acoustic guitar and male and female singers harmonizing on "da da da da" phrases. That tune made it through multiple rounds of vetting, according to Mr. Heard, before getting shot down by AT&T executives. Some listeners deemed it "too young" and "too Up With People," according to Beckerman's notes on the feedback. Beckerman said one of the most challenging aspects of the work was finding a common language to discuss it. "People would talk about the trumpets when there weren't any," he said, likening his role in such sessions as that of "musical shrink." His instruction: "Don't tell us what you want it to sound like; tell us how you want to feel when you hear it." Eventually his team landed on a core melody that stuck: a short phrase that seesaws through a series of octaves. But the results, when worked up as a full song with strings and synthesizers, seemed "too clean" and too corporate, Mr. Beckerman said. The solution: Man Made rented an old upright piano and a "messed up" glockenspiel. Players incorporated a woolly-sounding 1970s Wurlitzer keyboard and (after Beckerman stumbled on some Celtic rock on a music blog) bagpipes. The company's new sonic logo—its first—is a stair-step of bright tones. The bite-size tune has popped up in the closing seconds of the company's advertisements, including a TV spot in heavy rotation featuring a stolen tiger mascot and football tailgaters boasting about the speed of AT&T's wireless network. In various lengths and forms, the music will eventually be integrated into every product and service AT&T offers, from music at retail stores to navigation sounds on smartphones and digital video recorders.[2]

What are Beckerman's fondest memories of creating the AT&T sonic logo?

It's eight years in market. It took about 18 months to get there. Not that the work took 18 months but large organization, I think at the time, 230,000 employees. So it was quite a thing to sort of get up the food chain and get everybody bought in on these projects. Getting it bought in is half the battle because people don't feel invested in it. It's not going to end up across the brand, which is really the focus. So, I guess really one of the sort of most interesting elements of this often is to work and collaborate with the advertising agency that's a part of the project. So, David Lubars who's at BBDO, executive creative director, he was charged to work with me on this by Esther Lee at the time, the CMO of AT&T. And David came to my studio at one point and he was sort of listening to the work that was going on and we were talking about a bunch of the elements and we sort of pushing faders up and down. And David said, "How do you deconstruct this?" which I thought was a really interesting idea, which really is about simplifying. And as you might know from my book, my approach usually is to create a long form piece of music first and then distill it down, distill it down to its essence. So, in the recording studio, that's where we started pushing the faders up and down against that sonic logo. And David again had said, "What would be deconstructed?" So, really pulled down probably three quarters of the material that was there led more with one particular sound and had all the other sounds supporting that one sound. So there's that featured sound which almost has a kind of a popping sound to it. And that idea of sort of lining everything up, simplifying it, having one lead sounds and other sounds just in the perfect... really perfect, sort of like making a cocktail or certain tiny little bits of flavor in it and leading with some and pulling others back ended up being the solution along with a bunch of processing and equalization. I mean, we probably spent weeks really kind of finding that perfect combination of colors in the sounds with those notes. In a lot of ways, we think about the notes as being kind of half the battle in the sonic logos that are more melodic driven. The other is really thinking about the sounds themselves, so you want the notes to be somewhat iconic but also the sonics of that sonic logo to be iconic so that it passes what I call the ham sandwich factor, which is if you're in the kitchen making ham sandwich and you hear that advertisement on the television that you'll recognize it instantly.[3]

Did he work out from a couple of notes or did you go big and then deconstructed it down to just a series of notes?

So it all comes back to the assignment and the strategy and really what we're trying to accomplish. Brands are stories and we need to always understand what's the story we're trying to tell which leads us to different kinds of solutions. I think of themes for companies really much like a pop song. It's very much kind of a modular construction that there is sort of... I wouldn't say a formula. There're probably 50 formulas for a song but there are certain kinds of things you go from a verse to a chorus and maybe a bridge and then a half chorus. And then some other kind of element and then you end up with sort of a big recap of the chorus at the end, maybe repeating it two or three different times. So, there is a structure to a pop song and a great pop song and a lot of great songs fit that structure. The same thing is true with themes for brands. So, if we go back to the original ask, the original ask was, look, our problem is the network is amazing, the network makes an iPhone possible for instance, but the network is invisible. The phone you can hold in your hand, it's tangible, you can see it. So, when you're using a phone and everything's fine, you love the phone. And then when the network drops, you hate the network. So really, the network only got credit for the horrible experiences and none of the great experiences. So really the assignment was how do we remind people that AT&T is [inaudible 00:06:43] in making the iPhone work. And more importantly or just as importantly I guess, to recognize that it's not only sort of a big company or like a big dump pipe, but it actually, again, facilitates these things that you love. And it's very approachable. The idea was, again, not this big cold company, but really hearing the individuals and the people who are part of the process of making these things happen. So, that really was the beginnings of what the theme would be. And really what inspired us in terms of writing that theme is telling that story. And then as you suggested, a lot of times it's really hard to tell. It's like, "Oh, we're sending out to make notes?" We don't know. Is it going to be sonics only? Is it going to be a modular construction of different elements when we come back to sonic logo within perhaps if you imagine that a unique sonic or a sound effect along with notes that might work by itself or that may work together or those elements may work by themselves to be able to recognize the brand. The right solution for AT&T, again, we didn't go into this thinking this is the right solution, but it ended up being those four notes and a transitional device that got us from some other piece of content whether it was the end of a piece of advertising or the end of perhaps something like an outdoor activation or something in retail store and something in the phone actually created ringtones out of this. But the solution really ended up being that transitional sound which was somewhat iconic and recognizable by itself, but in combination with the notes really became iconic and endurable for them and that it's lasted eight years.[4]

Does he still think of these as brand anthems?

I've shifted from talking about anthem as really to talk about themes. And part of that is anthem has kind of threw people off a little bit, that terminology. So, we still do the same thing we did before. We're just using different terminology to help people understand better what it is that we're creating. So a theme is analogous to a theme for a movie or a theme for a television show and people start to get the idea that it is a story, a story to be told as compared to what we used to call this long form work which is an anthem. And people sometimes think of like the national anthem or it tends to be something a little more chest beating. So, we've shifted to now calling them themes. But, again, very much like a pop song, I've got to bring up that analogy again. You're going a lot of times and maybe you write the verse first and maybe there's some idea about the bridge and then you write the chorus, you rewrite the verse and then, "Ahh, the chorus isn't quite right" and you change some other piece of the chorus. When it all fits together, when it all, again, feels like that modular construction of a verse, a chorus, some kind of bridge and it feels right. Then I think what drops out of that is the sonic logo, which absolutely is analogous to the hook. What's interesting and sometimes can be a little challenging in the process, which is a good problem, is you end up sometimes with more than one hook. So maybe you might have a primary hook and a secondary hook. So, if you hear the theme, there is certainly (singing), which is the primary hook, but there's also this other element which is (singing), which essentially is an answer. But as we were creating it, we weren't quite sure which was going to be the primary hook. But, again, the first one I sang is very much the primary hook and that's what people remember which is an earworm.[5]

And what does he think of today when he hears it?

I think of the 18 months it took to put it together. No, actually, what I think of is that I'm proud that it's been around for a long time and that to me means that we were successful in creating something that had value, an ongoing value. I remember maybe four years into this process, maybe three and a half, the AT&T folks came back and said, "Look, we're not just a network now. We're really focusing on the fact that we're leaning into entertainment." They had bought a whole bunch of entertainment properties. Certainly, Warner being one of the biggest ones at the time and then they have certainly acquired many more since then. And it was really about focusing on this Footprint Entertainment that it wasn't just the means of distribution, the means of putting things out in the world, but actually the thing that you're putting out in the world, the entertainment, the thing that draws you, that pulls you in with the network being a facilitation of what that distribution is. And what we had to do was really evolve the sonic logo and create something that was more heartfelt, entertainment-oriented. So I think when you listen to the two of these logos, you'll definitely hear the difference where the first is more friendly and welcoming and the second definitely feels more evocative and emotional.[6]

Does he think that sonic logos are even more relevant today?

Well, there's certainly a lot to be said about the economy of the sonic logo. That that hook or that earworm as you talk about it is very economical. I believe the sonic logo for AT&T was about two and a half seconds. Some of them were even shorter like their expressive logos that happened with acoustic guitar for instance that I think were about a second and three quarters. So that economy of time, you think about for instance in advertising for sure, how much each second is worth from that 30-second or 60-second ad. So part of it is really just thinking about how valuable that real estate is and part of it is making sure that there's plenty of real estate in that commercial for the advertising agency to tell their story. So, more and more, I think about the sonic logo as sort of the linchpin for sonic identity or sonic identity system, which really is analogous with visual identity. So a visual identity is not just the mark. A visual identity is all the different elements that you can recognize and that are part of a storytelling in a visual logo. So you have color, you have shape, you have animation. There's a lot of different elements that make up a visual identity so that that brand can live in very organic way, in ways that are very consistent with the experiences you want to have everywhere. So whether it's South by Southwest or it turns out it's something at the beginning of, for instance, places where there are film festivals, places where, again as you mentioned, digital devices, things like Pay Sounds. So, each of those are derivative of or part of a sonic identity system that's inclusive of the sonic logo. Again, with the sonic logo being the linchpin. What we find is all these other elements, some of them are really direct derivatives, especially Pay Sounds, where you want to make that very, very close to or really pretty much identical to a sonic logo but really designed for a phone speaker. To things like what we call Brand Navigation Sounds which are UI sounds, user interface sounds, or user experience sounds that show up in a whole variety of devices, whether it's a baby monitor, whether it has to do with the electric cars or the future of autonomous vehicles that these sounds that are intuitive, it helps us understand the experiences we're having, again, tied back to the sonic logo which, again, really is the hero.[7]

Does he expect to see more brands use sonic branding?

Well, crystal ball says that fewer and fewer people are watching full length advertising. So, brands really need to show up in ways that are relevant to customers who are spending much more time online, who are spending much more time in this sort of... Again, right now, we're in an odd moment in the worlds, but usually it would be in places like football games or other kinds of stadium experiences. Again, having these sonic logos show up in ways that are relevant. Again, you would hate to have a sonic logo interrupt your football experience. Certainly, when there's a touchdown, that's not where you're going to have a big AT&T sonic logo. But what we did for the Dallas Cowboys, for instance, was to create a mashup of several different stadium rock songs where the logo was sort of included as really a variation of the logo in particular moments I'm thinking right now. It was really about using orchestral chimes which just was kind of like a fun, quirky way to hear the logo in tune, not only with the stadium rock, but also in tune with what you might want to hear in a celebration when your team gets a touchdown. So, these sounds are definitely more and more relevant. The sonic logos themselves are more and more relevant but we really have to be very smart now about how we incorporate those notes into the experiences. Again, that it doesn't stick out, it just belongs. It just feels like it's part of the experience rather than pasted on to the experience.[8]

So, Beckerman is a musician, would he give up all the audio branding for one sold out concert tour?

Yeah. I'd like to think that I'm still a musician and still a composer. I'll still do the ad television show here and there and maybe a little independent film. So I still love creating music. It's in my blood. It's certainly a first love of mine. So, yeah, it reminds me of... I'll just tell you a super quick story. So the whole birth of going into essentially creating sonic identity systems, which sounds so sterile, but actually it has so many different creative possibilities in ways it could show up. So, the birth of that whole idea, I was scoring a television show, the last episode of a particular season, and the audience that you get for that, the ratings you get for that really helps determine whether or not you're going to get a next season or they're going to cut a short season or the show could go away. So, I was working on this final episode and the showrunners and the script was wrong. The way they shot it was wrong. There were gaping holes in terms of really logic and story and performances and they kept sending me cut after cut after cut of this episode hoping that I'd be able to save it with music. And it's very difficult to really save something with music. You can improve it. So anyway, I'm looking at my seventh cut. I literally hadn't slept for about a week because they were close to delivery and I was staring at the seventh cut and I knew I was never going to make them happy. I remember saying at the screen, "I would like to be scoring anything else that's on this screen." And that idea sort of stuck. It's like, "Well, why don't I score the rest of the world and like what would that be like?" And that was really sort of the birth of this. And it's thrilling. I mean, you can create music for a television show or a film and it has a certain lifespan. Not to say that great films don't continue on forever, but strangely enough, the idea of the sonic identity systems, they just go on and on and on when you do it correctly. And it still is really fun to be able to hear those things out in the world, recognizing that there may be hundreds of millions of plays of these sonic identities. There are certain millions of plays with hundreds of millions of impressions each year. That's kind of fun to think about impacting an audience like that. For instance, there's some work that I did for the... Well, originally it was for the Super Bowl on NBC which became the NFL on NBC, which was based on a John Williams melody and it was really about extending that melody into a longer form. And how thrilling and exciting it was to be able to recognize that that music that I extended and created a brand new arrangement for was in front of, again, hundreds of millions of people in plays. That's always been super thrilling for me.[9]

So, other than AT&T, what's his favorite sonic logo?

I have to go with NBC. I mean, look in ubiquity of it and the fact that the network has committed to it for decades is so interesting. Recognizing that it originally started, there were these sort of little handheld chimes, which were used on the hour as a station ID, station identifier, and it was actually required at the time that if you had a broadcast network, you had to identify that network on the hour, every single hour. So, there's only a certain number of notes that are available in these little handheld chimes. If I remember correctly, it's a major chord. So, somebody came up with the idea of what that would be, essentially G, E, C. And the fact that that identifier went on for a number of years and then when those identifiers were no longer necessary that it carried through with the network for decades and decades after that. There've been so many reinterpretations of it that it still exists at the beginning of *The Today Show* for instance or a bunch of other shows or what they call promos which live next to advertising usually where you see an NBC logo. It's just fascinating to me. And so amazing that it's so ubiquitous and has lived such a long life.[10]

One final fun fact about the AT&T campaign?

I think that there was a group, actually that group is still together at Man Made. They were working on the sonics of the sonic logo for AT&T, again, for weeks and weeks and weeks, trying all sorts of different versions and variations and getting input from me and from the network... or excuse me, from the client and from the agency. And they would go through and create 30 different variations, same notes, but very, very different sonics. And then they get another series of notes and then they go back and work on it again and again and again and then again and again and again. And it must have been probably 15 different recording sessions until they got something that everyone bought off on. We called it the dream team, the dream team. We had to cut or lighten it up and make it fun for them and kind of make them special because you got to imagine sitting in a recording studio for that many weeks, that many versions and variations, it can drive you a little insane. It's sort of like drip, drip, drip, drip, drip in over time. And then one other fun fact is sometimes they would go create versions and variations and then the next morning they would say, "Yeah, these really aren't that different." They get so in tuned to that tiny, tiny, tiny little differences that when you show up in the morning is you recognized you really haven't made much progress.

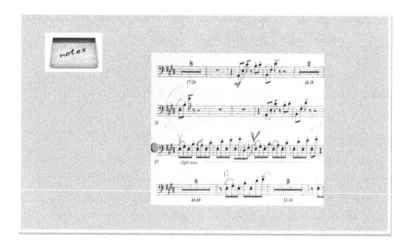

The Next Chapter

Mastercard (2019)

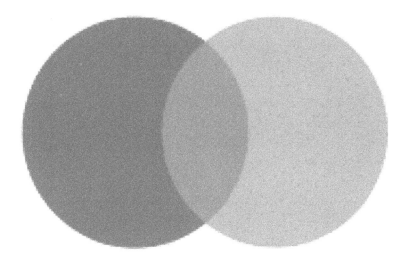

Destined to be classic but too early to be considered for the best of all time, the next chapter of sonic strategy and logos has to be Mastercard. The press release sounded the charge....

Setting a new tempo for brand expression, Mastercard debuts its sonic brand identity, a comprehensive sound architecture that signifies the latest advancement for the brand. Wherever consumers engage with Mastercard across the globe—be it physical, digital or voice environments—the distinct and memorable Mastercard melody will provide simple, seamless familiarity. The news comes on the heels of the company's recent transition to a symbol brand and is part of its continued brand transformation. "Sound adds a powerful new dimension to our brand identity and a critical component to how people recognize Mastercard today and in the future," said Raja Rajamannar, chief marketing and communications officer, Mastercard. "We set out an ambitious goal to produce the Mastercard melody in a way that's distinct and authentic, yet adaptable globally and across genres. It is important that our sonic brand not only reinforces our presence, but also resonates seamlessly around the world." To ensure the Mastercard melody would resonate with people the world over, Mastercard tapped musicians, artists and agencies from across the globe, including musical innovator Mike Shinoda of Linkin Park. The result, a distinct and memorable melody with adaptations across genres and cultures, making it locally relevant while maintaining a consistent global brand voice. In addition, the use of varying instruments and tempos help to deliver the Mastercard melody in several unique styles such as operatic, cinematic, and playful as well as a number of regional interpretations. The Mastercard melody is the foundation of the company's sound architecture and will extend to many assets, from musical scores, sound logos and ringtones, to hold music and point-of-sale acceptance sounds. "What I love most about the Mastercard melody, is just how flexible and adaptable it is across genres and cultures," said Mike Shinoda. "It's great to see a big brand expressing themselves through music to strengthen their connection with people." With voice shopping set to hit $40 billion by 2022, audio identities not only connect brands with consumers on a new dimension, they are tools enabling consumers to shop, live, and pay in an increasingly digital and mobile world. "Audio makes people feel things, and that's what makes it such a powerful medium for brands, said Matt Lieber", Cofounder and President, Gimlet. "With the explosion of podcasts, music streaming, and smart speakers, an audio strategy is no longer a "nice-to-have" for brands—it's a necessity. A sonic identity—the audio calling card for a brand—is now just as important as a brand's visual identity."[1]

Meet Raja Rajamannar. He is an accomplished global marketing executive with more than 25 years of experience, the last six of which have been in the role of Chief Marketing & Communications Officer for Mastercard and President of the company's healthcare business. Raja is consistently recognized globally as a highly innovative and transformational leader in his field. Some of his recent accolades include: Global Marketer of the Year award by the World Federation of Advertisers, top 5 "World's Most Influential CMOs" by Forbes, top 10 "World's Most Innovative CMOs" by Business Insider, and inductee to The CMO Club Hall of Fame. He has also been recognized as one of AdWeek's most tech-savvy CMOs.

**Chief Marketing & Communications Officer and President,
Healthcare, Mastercard**

He recently assumed the honorary role of President of the World Federation of Advertisers. Raja has also been recognized by ANA Educational
Foundation as the Marketer of the Year in 2019. At Mastercard, Raja
is responsible for successfully leading the company's marketing transformation, including the integration of the marketing and communication
functions, the development of its Priceless experiential platforms, and the
creation and deployment of cutting edge marketing-led business models
into the core of the company. Raja has overseen the successful evolu-
tion of Mastercard's identity for the digital age, pioneering Mastercard's
move to become a symbol brand and launching its breakthrough sonic
brand platform. Interbrand has ranked Mastercard as the fastest growing
brand across all industries and categories, worldwide in 2019. In his role
as President of Healthcare, Raja has overseen the creation, development,
and successful scaling of Mastercard's healthcare business across multiple

regions. Raja has been recognized for driving business transformation across a variety of geographies and industries, including consumer products, financial services and healthcare. Prior to Mastercard, he served as Chief Transformation Officer of the health insurance firm Anthem (formerly WellPoint), and served as Chief Innovation & Marketing Officer at Humana. Earlier in his career, Raja held senior management roles with Asian Paints, Unilever and Citibank. Raja is a member of the Board of Directors of PPL Corporation and Bon Secours Mercy Health and serves on the boards of the New York City Ballet, Cintrifuse, and ANA.

What's his background?

I'm originally from India. I was born and brought up there. I studied chemical engineering and I thought I'd take up a career in environmental engineering, but somewhere I strayed into marketing in my MBA. And since then I have been in the field of marketing, now for more than 35 years. I worked across multiple geographies in the world—India, Middle-East and Africa, Europe, United States, and global. So, I moved all over the place and I also worked in different industries. I started my career in the paints industry. After 3 years, I moved to consumer packaged goods, with Unilever. Then I moved to financial services and worked for 15 years with Citibank. Then I moved into healthcare where I spent about four years and then I moved into payments for the last seven years. I also serve on the board of directors of a couple of companies. One is PPL Corporation, which is a Fortune 500 power generation and distribution company, and the second one is Bon Secours Mercy Health, which is one of the largest not-for-profit hospital systems in the United States and Ireland.[2]

How did he end up as the CMO at Mastercard?

Well, I'm very grateful for my journey. Roughly half of my career I spent in marketing proper, and the other half was managing P&Ls and leveraging marketing, so marketing was reporting to me in my P&L roles. I was managing businesses or divisions or a company like Diners Club. So, it's been a very exciting journey and marketing is definitely my first love and something which I'm very deeply passionate about. I try to stay current, and I'm also writing a book on marketing, which I'm very excited about.

I just finished the manuscript. It's called *Quantum Marketing* and it all about the how marketing will be transformed in the immediate future and how marketers have to navigate that future to survive and thrive. The book will be released on February 9, 2021, and is already available now for preordering on Amazon and a bunch of other eCommerce sites.[3]

And does he consider himself a musician?

I don't know if I'm a musician, but I have deep appreciation of music. For a short while, I was classically trained in Carnatic music, which is South Indian classical music and I had learned it for about two and a half years. So that's not a whole bunch of time to learn classical music, but I grew up in a family of musicians. My mom was a very good singer, classical singer. Both my sisters used to sing classical Carnatic and my father used to play one of the percussion instruments called tabla. So I grew up listening to music and so it's a part of my DNA, but I really don't know if I'm qualified to call myself a musician.[4]

And was it his love for music that facilitated Mastercard's sonic branding strategy?

Yeah, it was definitely my brain child, I would say. Having got that sensibility around music, I always felt that music could be a very powerful component of marketing in general and branding in particular. And so, about 2013 or 2014, I can't exactly remember when, I started this effort—why don't we get music into our marketing mix and why don't we create a musical identity for our brand? So that effort we had embarked on and pursued for about two years. It did not go anywhere because the kind of complexities I was dealing with, it has to be universal, it has to be neutral, it has to fit every situation, it has to be applicable across all the geographies and all the genres, getting to the universally applicable and likeable musical notes and tune, etc. So after two years we just took a pause and again, restarted in 2016. And this time around, I started working with folks from the music industry, in a sense that I was working with musicians, musicologists, studios, of course our advertising agencies and music agencies. It was a pretty complex exercise and it took me two years this time as well. But this time, the two years were productive and we came up with a tune that was on the one hand pleasant, second it was simple. If it is complex it won't work in the marketing context. It had to be memorable. That which is not memorable, will not get associated anyway to the brand, so why even have it? We said it has to be hummable, hummable because that which you hum really sticks in your mind quite deeply. Then I said, it had to feel very native, whether you're playing that music in Dubai or in Shanghai or in Bogota or in Germany, it had to appeal universally, but also feel native. So you're not getting to the lowest common denominator, but you're going to the highest common factor, so to speak. Then we also said, it had to be native in different contexts. For example, we sponsor football and we sponsor ballet. Now, these are extremes in terms of the musical nature of the sound. And our melody has to be applicable in both these contexts. Then we said, we also have to be very situationally appropriate, like in a romantic evening setting or in a very noisy electronic dance music festival. It had to feel native in both the cases. So, when I gave this brief to the agency, they looked like I had multiple heads and I don't blame them. But eventually we kept on at it and working with so many folks and creating options, testing them out. So, for example, when a melody is created, we are going to check it in various countries and see if it is appealing or not. And then go back to the drawing board if it works in some areas, but not in some other areas. So it was a very long, very expensive journey, but something which I'm very grateful that we landed with a 30-second melody, which is basically at the core of our entire sonic branding. Now, even when we were developing this, my own thinking started evolving on it. I was looking at various companies, which have been exploring sonic branding and incorporating music into their marketing mix. So there were companies, for example, like Intel, which had a beautiful mnemonic at the end of their ads, they stuck to it consistently, and today you don't have to look at the screen, you just listen to that sound, and you recognize it as the mnemonic of Intel. British Airways has done it in a very different way. They created a beautiful melody, it was an aria and they were using it in all the places, whether it was on the plane or it was in their ads. That was a different kind of an approach. And of course you had McDonald's and you had NBC, you're got a whole bunch of companies which were leveraging

music in some form or fashion, but what was missing in the industry, to my mind, was that there was no comprehensive brand architecture. Like when you're designing your visual logo, you create a whole visual architecture, and a complete visual design system. But, nothing of that sort was available in the sonic space for audio branding. So we had to create our own playbook, based on our own sonic branding architecture. Our sonic branding architecture will have 10 different layers. And the first layer is the 30 second melody that I was talking to you about. Then the second layer is a three second subset of the 30-second melody, which is our mnemonic or the sonic signature. When you listen to it, you know that this is Mastercard. And we play our melody at all our events as background music, we use it in our advertisements, in our conferences, and our videos, it's all embedded there. We end all our ads with our sonic signature. Then the third layer is what we call as the acceptance sound. So in our case, unlike many of the brands you interact with, our brand comes into play each time you are making a payment with your credit card or debit card, either at a point of sale or online. That's an opportunity where consumers are looking for a confirmation that their transaction has gone through successfully. So we created a subset of the three seconds mnemonic into a 1.3 seconds sound. And that's what we released as our acceptance sound. We had to also be very careful that this acceptance sound did not create fatigue. Imagine, if you are a sales person or the checkout clerk at Walmart, hundreds of people are going by your checkout. And each time you are listening to the acceptance sound, you should not get tired of the at sound. So, we had to make sure that this was very well researched from a neurology point of view, from a fatigue point of view. I'm very happy to say that that sonic acceptance, the acceptance sound that we have is now live at more than 49 million points of interaction around the world. Well, I mean the easy thing would have been, you just sponsored a concert tour, you know that right? And a big logo in the back of the band, but it speaks to, I think, your appreciation of sonic branding, that it has to be all encompassing. And I think it also speaks to the fact that you understand that it's not just important for the customer that is using Mastercard, but in a lot of ways for the customer, who's not using Mastercard to get their attention and say, "Oh, are they using something I don't have that I should have?" kind of thing, which is brilliant, I think, in so many different levels.[5]

How's it going so far?

It's been very rewarding for us because already in a short period of one year, we have been rated as the world's best sonic brand, coming from behind. And there were other brands which were around for decades, invested in their sonic brand. So this thoughtful approach seems to be paying off. We're getting very good feedback from our customers and from our cardholders, which has been really good. And so there are more layers that are in the pipeline, which I cannot talk about right now. But rest assured that this is going to be a very long journey with multiple, multiple elements to our sonic branding that will be coming. And one of those, which we have also done earlier this year—we created a song, incorporating the Mastercard melody, not as a corporate anthem. If you play corporate anthem, people will throw up. It's not a corporate anthem, but leveraging the melody to create a popular song. The idea behind this is that I've came up with this three A's model. So first you need to create an awareness for the melody. The second a is an association between the melody and the brand, Mastercard. And the third a is attribution. When you ask people, they able to attribute this correctly to Mastercard. So basically these three A's, it's almost like a funnel. So if I have to now start making people recognize this melody, how do I do it? One of the best ways I can do it is by getting into the popular culture, by creating a song. And that song has got our melody, so people, while enjoying the song, they will start getting awareness of the melody. So we created our first song called Merry Go Round. Now we are at the verge of launching a full album, with 11 songs in it. Each one of them have got elements of the Mastercard melody incorporated in it, but they one doesn't sound repetitive. They're extremely diverse and very different. Music is so personal. You might love a particular kind of music, but I am not. So we had to really look at the aspect of incorporating melody into a multitude of songs. And each song may appeal to a different segment, different mindset of people. And so that's the journey that we are on right now and hoping to launch it before the end of the year, unless COVID comes back, which I hope it doesn't.[6]

Can you say to Alexa, "Alexa, use my Mastercard," and then hear the audio logo?

In fact, in some geographies you can. It's not across the board, but that's exactly the point. So what happens is it's not just smart speakers alone, but if you think of Internet of Things, meaning your connected refrigerator, your connected thermostat, your connected washing machine, any connected device will be a device for marketing. And when you talk of marketing, you need to show your brand there. So, for example, we have launched, over two years back, a pilot with Samsung to launch a refrigerator, a connected refrigerator. So the refrigerator senses which items are there in the refrigerator, and which are running out of stock, it'll automatically place a reorder. And the stocks will come to you from FreshDirect. So this is something which we had done. That was just a pilot kind of scenario, but this is going to happen and accelerate in future. Smart speakers are another brilliant example where the entire transaction happens through a voice, there has no visual real estate at all. So as a brand, how do you get into that stream of consciousness? Into that stream of sound? That's where sonic branding comes in, and becomes so incredibly important. And, for example, just 24 months back, or maybe even, say 18 months back, the penetration of smart speakers in the United States was 10 percent. By the end of 2019, it had shot up to 26 percent. It is amazing how fast it is growing. And this is only going to accelerate. You'll be talking to your, for example, thermostat. So you say, "Hey thermostat, reduce the temperature to 68" and it does. And it gives you a confirmation sound. That could be a Mastercard, if it is indeed relevant. So, you need to find the relevance. You need to find the occasion, you need to find the medium and showcase your brand. So particularly, if there is a purchase that is being made, Mastercard wants to always be there. There are 49 million places where you actually hear the audio brand of Mastercard, when you pay with your Mastercard and the transaction goes through successfully. So, when you go to a shop like Fred Segal's, you'll swipe your card or you tap your card at the sales terminal. As soon as the transaction has been approved, it plays the acceptance sound of Mastercard.[7]

What's the relationship between the audio and print logos?

So when we looked at our logo, we have two colors, red and yellow are the two circles, which are overlapping. Red, we call, is the color of passion. And yellow is the color of optimism. And we tried to bring those, the passion and optimism into all the depictions of our brand. So for example, in partnership with La Durée we created macarons—we call it the taste of Mastercard. So there is a taste of passion and there is a taste of optimism. And the second one is about optimism. Whether it is taste or sound, there is an upbeat or uplifting feel. So we try to sort of get these two components in, through everything that we do.[8]

What does he think of when he hears the sonic logo?

As a consumer, as a normal person, I find it pleasant. And it gives me a sense of completion. Like for example, when a transaction has gone through with my Mastercard and I hear that sound, it gives a sense of completion. It's gratification, it's satisfaction, a feeling that something has gone through safely. It's a peace of mind. That's one, as a consumer, as an individual. Likewise, as a consumer, or as an individual. I listened to Mastercard songs and they are very enjoyable. And now, if I put on the cap of a marketing guy and then listen to this, it's very gratifying. It's exactly delivering what we were hoping that it'll deliver, the right feelings, the right message, and the right characteristics to it, it has no fatigue, no tediousness etc. On the other hand, there is a sense of optimism, a sense of passion, a sense of completion and gratification. So they really work very well.[9]

Does he think the Mastercard sonic logo will be around as long as the NBC chimes?

I'm not saying it with a sense of arrogance, but I'm saying based on the amount of study we have done, the research we have done, the consumer feedback we have looked and worked with the best in the world, in the field of music. So there are a lot of indications that it's all going to be very successful. Just to give you an indication, but we were hoping that we will reach, within the first one year, probably about two to three million places through our sonic acceptance and here we are at 49 million! So it's taking off for us quite nicely. We see the consumer behavior: How does it get impacted by the sonic? It's been very positive. Okay, I'm not at Liberty to share the specific lifts that happen in consumer confidence and consumer's feelings toward the brand. And consumer's propensity to spend more in future with my card, as opposed to somebody else's card, it's pretty high. It's very positive. And also we are looking at different manifestations, like if you go to China today, it's fascinating. They created a card which makes music. So the card, when you tap it at a shop, instead of the sound coming from the point of sale terminal, the sound comes from the card itself. So we are looking at all kinds of ways in which sound can be brought in. If you go to Korea and you're going through the subway there, there are those turnstiles. So when you tap your card, it makes the Mastercard sonic acceptance sound because, your subway ticket is on Mastercard. Or if you go to New York and get into some of these taxis, after the ride is over and you're getting out, it gives you the sound of Mastercard.[10]

It's much more than a marketing strategy. It's a marketing musicology strategy right?

Absolutely. That's exactly right. And a couple of things, which I would also want to say, maybe it's a little bit of a detour, but significant research studies are showing that consumer's feelings and moods can be much more affected by sound than the other sense. It is connected to some primal aspects because of how the human brain has developed. When the human being heard a threatening sound, the primal brain kicks into action. And then he starts taking off to save himself. I've just given you a negative example, but on the positive side as well, you see people, when they listen to some extraordinary music that touches deeply, they cry, they don't cry because they're unhappy, but it is the tears of joy that flow. It's a very deep connection. If you can appropriately and authentically tap into those deep areas, I think brands can really embed themselves quite nicely in the consumer's hearts and minds.[11]

Any fun fact or story around Mastercard's sonic logo?

Yeah, actually, this is something which happened probably a few years back, five, six years back. I wasn't fully aware of what EDM was, electronic dance music. So one my team members said, oh, that's the fastest growing category of music, you must experience it. I said, yeah, sure thing. So we flew into Atlanta and outside of Atlanta there was a program that was happening called Tomorrow World, a gigantic event. And there were like tens of thousands of people gathered and apparently they listen to the music concerts the whole day, literally, and very early into the next morning. And for 5 days or so! So I went there and my experience, I would say, I could barely stand for 10 minutes. I said, this is so out of sync with my sensibilities. But, that's the beauty of diversity. There are tens of thousands of people who are having a ball of their life. And here I, who is thinking, my God, I can barely tolerate this for 10 minutes. I told my team I am done with it. But, having looked at the people, seeing how well they're enjoying the whole show, I said let's go ahead and sponsor EDM. So, now we sponsor more than 80 electronic dance music festivals around the world. And the interesting thing, David, is one of our sonic melody renditions is in an electronic dance music version. And it was done for us by none other than Mike Shinoda, who is a cofounder of Linkin Park.[12]

Last Note

The sonic logos you already knew.

Now you know some of the creators.

For some it is there legacy.

For others it is just one more thing.

Some where classically trained and others went to the School of Rock.

All paid homage to the NBC Chimes and to Intel.

And the backstage stories are "priceless" …Can you believe that Steven Spielberg credited the sonic logo from John Williams for at least 50 percent of the success of Jaws?

Or that Mike Post has Grammy Awards for L.A. Law, Hill Street Blues, and The Rockford Files but says the Law and Order sonic logo has a special place in his heart.

Walter Werzowa's first love was Beethoven but it was ABBA (S.O.S.) and Indeep (Last Nite A DJ Saved My Life) that led to five million in sales. Intel allowed him the opportunity to return to Austria and make his teachers proud, again.

These all are now in the Hall of Fame of sonic logos.

In the future, we will undoubtedly have trouble getting the Mastercard sonic logo out of our head. And it's possible that after watching The Adventures of Mark Twain on Netflix that sonic logo might end up as an earworm too.

How ironic.

NETFLIX

Notes

First Note

1. eMarketer (2020).
2. OC&C (2018).
3. Minsky and Fahey (2017).
4. Minsky and Fahey (2017).
5. Ciccarelli (2019).
6. AMA (2019).
7. Jackson (2003), p. 9.
8. Jackson (2003), p. 5.
9. Jackson (2003), p. 23.
10. Jackson (2003), p. 15.
11. Bronner (2009), p. 78.
12. Renard (2017).
13. Jackson (2003), p. 9.
14. Jackson (2003), p. 9.
15. Krishnan, et al. (2012).
16. van Leeuwen (2017), p. 119.
17. van Leeuwen (2017), p. 120.
18. van Leeuwen (2017), p. 131.
19. Beckerman (2014), p. 8.
20. Jackson (2003), p. 23.
21. Treasure (2011), pp. 172–173.
22. Kellaris (2001).

Chapter 1

1. The "sound mark" registration expired on November 3, 1992. A second registration was made in 1971.
2. (15 U.S. Code § 1127)
3. U.S. Department of Commerce agency responsible for issuing trademark registration for product and intellectual property identification.
4. https://uspto.gov/trademark/soundmarks/trademark-sound-mark
5. Statement of Robert C. Wright, President and Chief Executive Officer. "National Broadcasting Company, Inc." Television Network Mergers Hearings before the Subcommittee on Telecommunications and Finance

of the Committee on Energy and Commerce, House of Representatives, One hundredth Congress, first session, April 28, 29, and 30, 1987, Volume 4, page 180.

6. The NBC chimes sound mark is currently assigned to NBCUniversal Media, LLC.

7. https://trademarks.justia.com/723/49/n-a-72349496.html

8. General Electric Broadcasting Co., 199 U.S.P.Q. 560, 562–563 (T.T.A.B. 1978).

9. Shoshani (n.d.).

10. Ellerbee (2017).

Chapter 2

1. Barkan (2015).

2. Burlingame (2012).

3. http://johnwilliams.org/reference/biography

4. Ross (2020).

Chapter 3

1. https://en.wikipedia.org/wiki/Deep_Note

2. https://uspto.gov/trademark/soundmarks/trademark-sound-mark-examples

3. http://jamminpower.org/index.html

4. Brownlee (2015).

5. Interview with Dr. James "Andy" Moorer (April 24, 2020).

6. Interview with Dr. James "Andy" Moorer (April 24, 2020).

7. Interview with Dr. James "Andy" Moorer (April 24, 2020).

8. Interview with Dr. James "Andy" Moorer (April 24, 2020).

9. Interview with Dr. James "Andy" Moorer (April 24, 2020).

10. Interview with Dr. James "Andy" Moorer (April 24, 2020).

11. Interview with Dr. James "Andy" Moorer (April 24, 2020).

12. Interview with Dr. James "Andy" Moorer (April 24, 2020).

13. Interview with Dr. James "Andy" Moorer (April 24, 2020).

14. Interview with Dr. James "Andy" Moorer (April 24, 2020).

Chapter 4

1. https://en.wikipedia.org/wiki/Law_%26_Order#Music_and_sound_effects

2. http://mike-post.com/biography/

3. https://en.wikipedia.org/wiki/Mike_Post

4. Genzlinger (n.d.).
5. Interview with Mike Post (April 24, 2020).
6. Interview with Mike Post (April 24, 2020).
7. Interview with Mike Post (April 24, 2020).
8. Interview with Mike Post (April 24, 2020).
9. Interview with Mike Post (April 24, 2020).
10. Interview with Mike Post (April 24, 2020).
11. Interview with Mike Post (April 24, 2020).

Chapter 5

1. Whitwell (2005).
2. Kaufman (1999).
3. Kaufman (1999).
4. Jackson (2003, p. 2).
5. See Intel Inside Making of the Music (2018).
6. https://en.wikipedia.org/wiki/Edelweiss_(band).
7. Interview with Walter Werzowa (April 22, 2020).
8. Intel (2014).
9. Intel (2014).
10. Interview with Walter Werzowa (April 22, 2020).
11. Kaufman (1999).
12. Kaufman (1999).
13. Interview with Walter Werzowa (April 22, 2020).
14. Intel (2014).
15. Sanders (2016).
16. Interview with Walter Werzowa (April 22, 2020).
17. Interview with Walter Werzowa (April 22, 2020).
18. Interview with Walter Werzowa (April 22, 2020).
19. Interview with Walter Werzowa (April 22, 2020).
20. Interview with Walter Werzowa (April 22, 2020).

Chapter 6

1. Frere-Jones (2014).
2. Selvin (1996).
3. https://bbc.co.uk/programmes/b00k3x21
4. Van Leeuwen (2017).
5. Eno (1975).
6. Van Leeuwen (2017).

Chapter 7

1. Marsden (2014).
2. https://linkedin.com/in/lancemassey/
3. Interview with Lance Massey (April 28, 2020).
4. Interview with Lance Massey (April 28, 2020).
5. Interview with Lance Massey (April 28, 2020).
6. Interview with Lance Massey (April 28, 2020).
7. Interview with Lance Massey (April 28, 2020).
8. Interview with Lance Massey (April 28, 2020).
9. Interview with Lance Massey (April 28, 2020).
10. Interview with Lance Massey (April 28, 2020).
11. Interview with Lance Massey (April 28, 2020).
12. Interview with Lance Massey (April 28, 2020).
13. Interview with Lance Massey (April 28, 2020).
14. Interview with Lance Massey (April 28, 2020).
15. Interview with Lance Massey (April 28, 2020).
16. Interview with Lance Massey (April 28, 2020).

Chapter 8

1. Elliot (2003).
2. White and Leung (2003).
3. Ives (2004).
4. Interview with Bill Lamar (June 24, 2020).
5. Interview with Bill Lamar (June 24, 2020).
6. Interview with Bill Lamar (June 24, 2020).
7. Interview with Bill Lamar (June 24, 2020).
8. Interview with Bill Lamar (June 24, 2020).
9. Interview with Bill Lamar (June 24, 2020).
10. Interview with Bill Lamar (June 24, 2020).

Chapter 9

1. Moye (2013).
2. Coca-Cola (2016).
3. https://linkedin.com/in/umut-ozaydinli-0896573/
4. https://linkedin.com/in/joe-belliotti-9977161/
5. Interview with Umut Ozaydinli and Joe Belliotti (May 01, 2020).
6. Interview with Umut Ozaydinli and Joe Belliotti (May 01, 2020).
7. Interview with Umut Ozaydinli and Joe Belliotti (May 01, 2020).

8. Interview with Umut Ozaydinli and Joe Belliotti (May 01, 2020).
9. Interview with Umut Ozaydinli and Joe Belliotti (May 01, 2020).
10. Interview with Umut Ozaydinli and Joe Belliotti (May 01, 2020).
11. Interview with Umut Ozaydinli and Joe Belliotti (May 01, 2020).
12. Interview with Umut Ozaydinli and Joe Belliotti (May 01, 2020).
13. Interview with Umut Ozaydinli and Joe Belliotti (May 01, 2020).
14. Interview with Umut Ozaydinli and Joe Belliotti (May 01, 2020).

Chapter 10

1. https://linkedin.com/in/joel-beckerman-93725/
2. Jurgensen (2012).
3. Interview with Joel Beckerman (May 24, 2020).
4. Interview with Joel Beckerman (May 24, 2020).
5. Interview with Joel Beckerman (May 24, 2020).
6. Interview with Joel Beckerman (May 24, 2020).
7. Interview with Joel Beckerman (May 24, 2020).
8. Interview with Joel Beckerman (May 24, 2020).
9. Interview with Joel Beckerman (May 24, 2020).
10. Interview with Joel Beckerman (May 24, 2020).
11. Interview with Joel Beckerman (May 24, 2020).

The Next Chapter

1. https://mastercardcontentexchange.com/newsroom/press-releases/2019/february/sound-on-mastercard-debuts-sonic-brand/
2. Interview with Raja Rajamannar (August 5, 2020).
3. Interview with Raja Rajamannar (August 5, 2020).
4. Interview with Raja Rajamannar (August 5, 2020).
5. Interview with Raja Rajamannar (August 5, 2020).
6. Interview with Raja Rajamannar (August 5, 2020).
7. Interview with Raja Rajamannar (August 5, 2020).
8. Interview with Raja Rajamannar (August 5, 2020).
9. Interview with Raja Rajamannar (August 5, 2020).
10. Interview with Raja Rajamannar (August 5, 2020).
11. Interview with Raja Rajamannar (August 5, 2020).
12. Interview with Raja Rajamannar (August 5, 2020).

References

"American Marketing Association." 2019. https://ama.org/publications/Marketing News/Pages/language-of-audio-branding.aspx

Barkan, J. June 17, 2015. "The Two Notes that Changed Horror Music Forever." *Bloody-disgusting.com*, https://bloody-disgusting.com/news/3349605/jaws-week-two-notes-changed-horror-music-forever/

Beckerman, J. 2014. *The Sonic Boom*, NY: Houghton Mifflin Harcourt.

Brownlee, J. April 08, 2015. "Behind The Redesign of the THX Deep Note, The World's Most Iconic Audio Logo." *Fast Company*, https://fastcompany.com/3044783/behind-the-redesign-of-the-thx-deep-note-the-worlds-most-iconic-audio-logo

Burlingame, J. August 21, 2012. "The Music of Jaws: An Interview With John Williams, Limelight." Available https://limelightmagazine.com.au/features/the-music-of-jaws-an-interview-with-john-williams/

Bronner, K. 2009. "Jingle all the way? Basics of Audio Branding." In *Audio Branding*, ed. Bronner, K. Germany: Nomos.

Ciccarelli, D. January 30, 2019. "If You're Going to Focus On One Thing this Year, Make it Audio Branding." *AdAge*, https://adage.com/article/voices.com/focus-thing-year-make-audiobranding/316418

Coca-Cola. 2016. "Taste the Felling." https://coca-cola.ie/marketing/campaigns/iconic/taste-the-feeling

Ellerbee, B. 2017. "November 29, 1929…The NBC Chimes Sound For The First Time." *Eyes Of A Generation…Television's Living History*, https://eyesofageneration.com/november-29-1929-the-nbc-chimes-sound-for-the-first-time/

Elliott, S. June 12, 2003. "McDonald's Campaign Embraces a Loving Theme." *The New York Times*, https://nytimes.com/2003/06/12/business/the-media-business-advertising-mcdonald-s-campaign-embraces-a-loving-theme.html

eMarketer. February 04, 2020. "Purchases Via Smart Speakers Are Not Taking Off." https://emarketer.com/content/purchases-via-smart-speakers-are-not-taking-off

Eno, B. 1975. *Liner notes for Discreet Music*. London: EG Records Ltd. http://eno-web.co.uk/discreet-txt.html (accessed May, 2020).

Frere-Jones, S. July 30, 2014. "Ambient Genius." *The New Yorker*, https://newyorker.com/magazine/2014/07/07/ambient-genius?reload=true?reload=true

Genzlinger, N. August 08, 2017. "Have you Heard This?" *New York Times*, https://nytimes.com/interactive/2017/08/13/arts/law-and-order-sound.html

Intel Inside Making of the Music - Walter Werzowa at beatvyne's MxT. 2019. https://.youtube.com/watch?v=LlmiuKehR8g

Intel. August 06, 2014. "Intel Bong Still Going Strong After 20 Years." https://newsroom.intel.com/editorials/intel-bong-chime-jingle-sound-mark-history/#gs.3uy94j

Ives, N. May 13 2004, "For McDonald's the 'I'm Lovin' It' Phrase of its New Campaign has Crossed Over into the Mainstream." *The New York Times*, https://nytimes.com/2004/05/13/business/media-business-advertising-for-mcdonald-s-m-lovin-it-phrase-its-new-campaign-has.html

Jackson, D.M. 2003. *Sonic Branding*. New York, NY: Palgrave Macmillan.

Jurgensen, J. January 28, 2012. "Making an Impression in Just Four Notes." *Wall Street Journal*, https://wsj.com/articles/SB100014240529702037185045771 82951405815364

Kaufman, L. October 20, 1999. "The Man Who Created Intel's Audio 'Signature'." *Los Angeles Times*, https://latimes.com/archives/la-xpm-1999-oct-20-fi-24321-story.html

Kellaris, J.J. Winter, 2001. "Identifying Properties of Tunes That Get 'Stuck in Your Head." *Proceedings of the Society for Consumer Psychology*, 66–67, Scottsdale: American Psychological Society.

Krishnan, V., J.J. Kellaris, and T.W. Aurand. 2012. "Sonic Logos: Can Sound Influence Willingness to Pay?" *Journal of Product & Brand Management* 21, no. 4, pp. 275–284.

Lindstrom, M. February 22, 2010. "The 10 Most Addictive Sounds in the World." *Fast Company*, https://fastcompany.com/1555211/10-most-addictive-sounds-world

Marsden, R. March 08, 2014. "Sonic Boom: Advertising is Increasingly Making Use of Tiny Tunes to Catch Our Attention." *Independent*, https://independent.co.uk/artsentertainment/music/features/sonic-boom-advertising-is-increasingly-making-use-of-tiny-tunes-to-catch-our-attention-9172004.html

Mastercard. February 08, 2019. "Sound On: Mastercard Debuts Sonic Brand." https://newsroom.mastercard.com/press-releases/sound-on-mastercard-debuts-sonic-brand/

Minsky, L., and C. Fahey. 2017. *Audio Branding*. UK: Kogan Page Limited.

Moye, J. July 15, 2013. "5 Facts About Coke's 5-Note Melody." *Coca-Cola Journey*, https://coca-colajourney.co.nz/stories/5-facts-about-cokes-5-note-melody

OC&C. February 28, 2018. "Voice Shopping Set to Jump to $40 Billion By 2022." *Rising From $2 Billion Today*. https://prnewswire.com/news-releases/voice-shopping-set-to-jump-to-40-billion-by-2022-rising-from-2-billion-today-300605596.html

Passman, J. November 02, 2016. "Intel, Netflix, Apple and the Power and Influence of Sonic Branding." *Forbes*, https://forbes.com/sites/jordanpassman/2016/11/02/intel-netflix-apple-and-the-power-and-influence-of-sonic-branding/#1c21f9a54836

Renard, S. March, 2017. "What Defines an Audio Logo? Composition and Meaning, College Music Dymposium." https://symposium.music.org/index.php/57/item/11341-what-defines-an-audio-logo-composition-and-meaning

Ross, A. July 21, 2020. "The Force is Still Strong with John Williams." *New Yorker*, https://newyorker.com/culture/persons-of-interest/the-force-is-still-strong-with-john-williams

Sanders, J.W. 2016. "Creative Review: Musikvergnuegen." *The Daily Brief, Promax*, https://brief.promax.org/content/creative-review-musikvergnuegen

Selvin, J. June 02, 1996. "Q and A With Brian Eno." *SFGate.com* https://sfgate.com/default/article/Q-and-A-With-Brian-Eno-2979740.php

Shoshani, M. "WSB Atlanta—Precursor to the NBC Chimes?" *The NBC Chimes Museum*, http://nbcchimes.info/radiochimes.php

Treasure, J. 2011. *Sound Business*. UK: Management Books.

van Leeuwen, T. 2017. "Sonic Logos." In *Music as Multimodal Discourse*, eds. Lyndon, C.W. and Simon, M., (Bloomsbury Advances in Semiotics, pp. 119–134). London: Bloomsbury Academic. http://dx.doi.org/10.5040/9781474264419.ch-006

Visa. ,2018. "Visa Brings Sensory Branding to Merchants, Terminal Manufacturers and Developers." https://usa.visa.com/about-visa/newsroom/press-releases.releaseId.15396.html

White, E., and S. Leung. August 06, 2003. "How a Tiny German Ad Agency Landed McDonald's Campaign." *Wall Street Journal*, https://wsj.com/articles/SB106011073587598800

Whitwell, T. 2005. "Tiny Music Makers: Pt 1: The 'Intel Inside' Chimes." Music Thing, https://musicthing.blogspot.com/2005/05/tiny-music-makers-pt-2-microsoft-sound.html

About the Author

David Allan, PhD, is the chair and professor of Marketing at Saint Joseph's University in Philadelphia, PA. Allan has a BA in Communications from American University; an MBA in Marketing from St Joes; and a PhD in Mass Media and Communication from Temple University. He has written two books (*This Note's For You* (Business Experts Press) and *HitPlay*); three book chapters (*Oxford Handbook of Music and Advertising* (in press), *Brick & Mortar*, and *Encyclopedia American Music and Culture*); six music case studies (David Bowie, Pepsi, JT, Taylor Swift, Beyoncé, and Coca-Cola); and has multiple journal articles (*Journal of Consumer Research, Journal of Business Research,* and *Journal of Advertising Research*) and a popular website (www.marketingmusicology.com). Prior to academia he spent 20+ years in radio as a DJ in Oxford, Ohio (97X) then Maryland, Virginia, and Pennsylvania as Program Director, Operations Manager, Regional Vice-President, Vice-President/General Manager (Power 99FM), and Senior Vice-President (Tak Communications, Evergreen Media, Chancellor Media and Clear Channel Communications, and iHeartmedia).

Index

Letter '*f*' after page number indicates figures.